YAHWEH:

His Fingerprints

are Everywhere

by

Judy Everswick

Yahweh: His Fingerprints are Everywhere

© 2022 Judy Everswick

Published in 2022 by Judy Everswick

ISBN: 978-0-578-28038-7

Contact the author at: zimbi7@gmail.com

Cover and interior design by Alane Pearce of Pearce Writing Services, LLC. apearcewriting@gmail.com

Thank you to Carolyn Kennedy for your hard work editing these stories.

Cover photo credit Braden Leif Everswick

All other photos the property of Judy Everswick

Dedication

I give thanks to THE ONE who has always had HIS finger-prints on my life. I am thankful to God for HIS constant presence. My life would have been very, very different if God had not prompted Ann Pape to walk across the street to share God's love with me and pointed to God's fingerprints on my life.

Lynn, I want to thank God for the privilege of walking by your side these last 55 years and being involved as partners in ministry. Next to my dependence on God, you have always been my rock and the one faithfully holding the rope as I ventured out. I love you.

To our amazing children and grandchildren, I thank God for each one of you and the spouses God has given you. You have brought so much joy to my life. Being your Mom and Gigi has been the most amazing privilege ever!

To each of the people represented in these stories, I want you to know how your commitment to God has impacted my life. There is so much more to your life than I could capture in these pages. I started writing because of a desire to share your stories. You are serving the Lord faithfully in your corner of the world. Your lives have Glorified God. I wanted others to hear a little about you. There are so many more who's paths have crossed mine, whose stories I could also have shared. I thank God for you.

Naming names is always challenging because I have been blessed by so many who have been true cheerleaders in putting these stories together: Pat, Bette, Denise, Liz, Carolyn, Sheryl, JoAnn, Danny, Jeff and so many others through the years who wanted to hear more about these heroes and saints we have met in our years of serving God.

Alane, thank you, for the huge push to get me to write and preserve the stories of these heroes of faith. How many times did I "close the computer" thinking that I'm not a writer, but I did so love sharing these stories of God's heroes, as well as the path that God has led us on through the years.

To those who might be taking the time to read these ramblings, I thank you. I pray that you might be encouraged to know how many are faithfully serving God in some challenging places, but they serve with JOY and FAITHFULNESS.

Philippians 4:8

About the Author

Judy Everswick is a life-long "missionary" focusing on sharing the love of God with people all over the world. She and her husband, Lynn, had the privilege of serving in Zimbabwe for a little over 14 years until Lynn was asked to return to the USA to serve as an Area Director for The Evangelical Alliance Mission for West Asia, and countries in Africa. In 1998, Lynn accepted the position as the first Global Pastor for Westover Church in Greensboro, North Carolina where he and Judy served for 17 years. In 2017 they retreaded and moved to Texas. They feel blessed to be living very close to three of their five children and have become an active part of the Lakeway Church in Lakeway, Texas.

Three Generations of The Everswick Family

Kimberly's Family: Chase, David, Kim, Titus, Luke, Lizzie, Colvin

Rick's Family: Max, Rick, Emily, Riley Anne

Brad's Family: Braden and Brad

Tim's Family: Back row L to R: Wyatt, Kendall, Jenn
Front row L to R: Tim, Austin, Kaylee

Brendon's Family: Lucas, Brendon, Aydan, Madia

What People are Saying About the Book

In the twenty-three years that we have known Lynn and Judy, they have been such an encouragement to us as well as literally hundreds of other missionary families all over the world! We have shared several adventures on the Amazon River, one of which you will read about in this book. Few people have done more to promote missions, or to make missionaries feel like they are a part of their immediate family! *--Kim and Rick Parker (Serving in Brazil)*

Hearing about believers on the other side of the world who have the same love and devotion to the Father as I do is like learning about a long-lost sister or brother you didn't know you had. What are their lives like? How can I love and pray for them? Should I go visit, get to know them better? What are their struggles? How can I support and encourage them? It is amazing how this connection as family overrides all differences of culture and ethnicity, and how a genuine love can be born, one that can only come from the bond of brotherhood. *--Debbie Deline*

The longer I walk with the Lord the more I want my heart to be burdened by the things that matter most to Him. I know from James 1:27 that God is deeply concerned about the plight of orphans. My time in Zimbabwe, serving alongside Garikai, Virginia, Lucy, and Judy with a team, afforded me the privilege of witnessing and experiencing firsthand what it looks like to love God in faith and obedience through loving these precious children. As a result to this day I am able to support them through prayer, time, and I am thankful for the impact that ministry made on my life. *--Sara Rogers*

In anticipation of my first mission trip, I can remember thinking that my main purpose or goal was to go and serve those who found themselves in situations less fortunate than I, which on some level might not have been totally incorrect, but God had so much more! I hope those with whom I interacted did feel loved and served, but, without a doubt, I was the one being welcomed and loved with humble hospitality, blessed beyond measure by seeing faith that seemed to know no bounds, and seeing joy in the Lord demonstrated regardless of circumstance. I am sure I received more from 'my going' than those we were 'going to' – a life-changing experience. *--Rebecca Pittard*

Judy's stories took me on her missionary journeys! I could see the people she met as though I was right there! Like the boy who made weights out of empty bottles. Or when Judy and Kim were scrubbing their feet and found a brush in a shower, not too savory, but it did the job! At the moment I read it, I was scrubbing my feet with you! The sights, tastes, sounds, "gut checks" were all emotions and word pictures I shared with you! This is not a story filled with boring slides and numbers or missionary letters tacked on a bulletin board filled with facts. Judy's stories left us wanting more! As a result, I woke up to pray for her often! She was on other side of world, but the stories made us feel like we were right there! The genius of the writing grabbed me!
This book will be devoured like delicious treats!!!! *--Elizabeth Milton*

Table of Contents

Foreword

The stories recorded here are about just a few of the heroes of our faith, faithfully serving God in their corner of the world. (Many of their names have been changed for their protection in closed countries.) There are so many more that could still be recorded.

Often as we visit countries we have experienced the same feelings that Lynn did when he first visited "The River City" back in 1983. *How will they hear about Jesus? Who will go and share the good news in places where they have never heard?*

Our children and grandchildren are athletes. We have spent a lot of our lives on the sidelines of various sports. Repeatedly we have seen that ball games are won in the last quarter. Sometimes the win/loss is actually decided in the last minutes. Lynn and I are in the last quarter of our lives. We feel more than ever, that it is important that we stay active until HE calls us home and that is our prayer for the next generation.

May all who come behind us find us faithful.

Introduction
God's Fingerprint on My Life

There are few things in life that are more intriguing to a little girl than being told that under no circumstances must you ever open this box. Curiosity can be almost palpable. The small, gray steel box was in the top right-hand drawer of my mom's desk upstairs. It was not really hidden from sight; it was right there in her desk, but the tone of voice that my mom used, and the stern look that my dad had when they warned me let me know, in no uncertain terms, that I was not going to disobey.

Christmas was different. My mom usually wrapped presents and hid them all over the house. Bright, shiny wrapped gifts were hidden in closets or under beds. More than once curiosity overcame me and I would look around the house for those boxes. I would ever so carefully slit the sticky tape with a sharp knife and slide the hidden treasure out of the paper to see what it was and who it was for. Then I would just as carefully get the box back into the wrapping paper and put fresh new tape on the corners

Sometimes the gift was for me--sometimes for one of my brothers, but the excitement of the hunt never faded. My mom, who had shopped for so many months and hiding those gifts, would wonder on Christmas Eve: "I thought that I had another gift for Tom (or George or Judy)." Then I could be the helpful elf. "Mom, I think it might be in the bedroom closet or under your bed." I was the hero!

However, I was never even tempted to open the gray box. Living in a his/hers/our family always piqued my curiosity: we did not know the whole story about our blended family. In the 1940's it was common to keep secrets about some of the details of one's past. I wondered about the who/how/why of our blended family, but never a word was spoken about either of my parents' former marriages, or what child belonged to whom.

There was a mini crisis when my middle brother wanted to quit high school and join the army during the Berlin Crisis. The scene is still fresh in my mind. George was only 17. He needed his birth certificate as well as my parents' permission to join the Army. Uncomfortable with the conversation, and obviously not ready to make any declarations, my parents' only reply was that they did not have a birth certificate for him. He insisted they must, and a big argument ensued.

I am not sure how or why my dad gave in, but I watched as he slowly and deliberately, but with a heaviness that I rarely had seen in him, headed up the stairs. A while later, he came down and handed George his birth certificate. It was that little white piece of paper that changed his life forever.

He asked my dad where he had found the birth certificate they said was lost? Why had he been hiding it? Where had he been hiding it?

As my brother read the information on the certificate, he was incredulous. Our mom was not his mom? Had he been deceived all his life? Where was his mom? What happened to her? Why did he not know about this? The fuse on my brother's temper was always very short. I so clearly remember the fighting that started between my dad and my brother. George started shouting, and he began beating up on my dad with anger and frustration. The burning tears running down the cheeks of Mom and Dad and my brother too are a visual that I will never forget. There was mayhem in the kitchen as my dad attempted explanations. I can remember sitting on the sofa, sad and confused and actually afraid for my dad's life with my brother hitting him with all his strength. I don't know which emotion was harder: the fear for my dad, who stood without retaliating; or my confusion over information that had been hidden from us for so many years.

I wondered at that time where my dad had found the birth certificate. Was that one of the things in the gray box in mom's desk? Were there other secrets hidden in the gray box? Would we ever know the answers about George's mom? Even with these questions, I never was tempted to open that box. Perhaps I was wondering if there were other secrets in there that I would rather not know.

Each of my older brothers had a different last name, so as I grew older, I guessed that they also had a different dad. A few times in my teens, I gingerly asked about these "other parents," but my parents were never forthcoming. I tucked these secrets away in my heart, but I was so loved by my parents and trusting of them, that I just decided that I didn't really want to know more.

In retrospect, I have seen God's fingerprints on my life even from that early age. The gray box was always a mystery growing up, but opening it was a line that I did not attempt to cross.

1

Called to Serve

My earliest childhood memories, with the exception of my brother's discovery, were mostly extremely happy ones. My dad was a tugboat captain in NY Harbor, following the profession of my paternal grandfather who was a Harbor Pilot who was called when there were big ships that needed to enter NY Harbor. My two brothers followed in the same profession. Dad would be gone two weeks at a time on the boat and then be home for a week. He bartended during his week at home. On those weekends we were in the bar all day with Dad. We were the "bartender's cute little kids" that everyone plied with cherry cokes and snacks all weekend. It was fun.

My parents and siblings were not church goers. We lived across the street from a German lady, Ann Pape, who asked my parents if she could take us to church. My parents were happy for us to go with her. I loved the church, the music, and the friends I met there, some of whom are friends 70 years later. It was there that I first heard about a God who loved me so much that He sent His son to die for me. God's grace was explained, and I accepted that grace eagerly. In my high school years, I got more involved in activities at the church and loved the opportunities to tell people about Jesus's love...for me and them. At 15, I became a follower of Jesus's teachings. I read vociferously stories of missionaries who served God with all their heart.

As a 16-year-old I was at a meeting at our church when a lady talked about the need for people to go and tell the people living in Africa about Jesus's love. She fervently shared that in America, people could hear about God in churches on almost every street corner or on TV and radio. In bookstores there were Bibles and literature about God. In the vast continent of Africa, there were thousands of Africans who had never once heard the name of Jesus. My heart was warmed and challenged thinking of those who never had the chance to hear about Christ and all that He had done for us. I knew at that very moment what I wanted to do when I graduated college. I shared that plan with my parents, and they smiled with acceptance, but they themselves did not understand or grasp God's love. They were quite sure that this was just a phase their little girl was going through.

Through the years at church growing up I had heard many people share their testimony. They spoke confidently of telling God that they would do anything to serve Him—just not in Africa, for example–yet, that's where they would end up serving. I was immature in my faith, but I wanted to have a testimony like those wonderful people of God. It seemed natural that I should apply to nursing school for my post high school training because, in my thinking, it was one thing I knew I didn't want to do for God. I really didn't want to be a nurse, but I filled out all the applications. I got my references and mailed that big fat envelope applying to the nursing college in downtown New York. Assuming that God would rather I went to Africa, I felt like I was well on my way to having a really neat testimony like some of the missionary giants that I had met or read about.

While I was waiting for what I was so sure would be an acceptance letter, I started reading missionary biographies. I read books that were written after the murder of five missionaries in Ecuador. One book in particular that moved me was The Dayuma Story. I never forgot her story nor her face.

The books I read and stories I heard spurred me on. I was ready to serve Him, even if it meant giving my life as a sacrifice for Him. "Greater love has no one that this to lay down one life for another." John 15:13. That was both a challenge and a joy for me. I was ready.

I was not ready for the rejection letter from the nursing school. Math and science were my two worst subjects in high school; how important those courses were to be a nurse! Now what? Was I not going to have an amazing testimony for Jesus someday?

Since my plan to go to nursing school didn't pan out, I considered airline school. I thought being a flight attendant would be cool. I knew that my parents would not have the money to send me to Bible college, so Plan B was to be trained as a flight attendant, work for a few years, save money, and when I had enough, go to Bible college to train for the mission field. I applied and was accepted.

Every summer in high school and college I worked at a camp in upstate New York with special-needs children. The summer after graduating from high school, I was working at Camp Hope, and a young man who was the son of the director asked me what I was going to do now that I had finished high school. I told him my plan about becoming a flight attendant so I could make enough money to pay my Bible college. His response really impacted me. "Judy, I know that you don't have money to go to college, but if you are going to live the rest of your life by faith, serving God in Africa, don't you think that you should start living by faith now?" He told me about a Bible college that sounded like what I wanted. I decided to apply and never looked back at the job with the airline. I was accepted to the college and started there the following fall.

***

The years at Bible college were amazing, but the most amazing happening was that on the first day of school, I met my soul mate, Lynn Everswick. Lynn's and my backgrounds are vastly different. Lynn was brought up as a missionary kid in Africa, and I, as the daughter of a tugboat captain in New York Harbor. But our commitment to serving God was the same.

Lynn's desire to return to the mission field came as a result of seeing the need for people to serve in a cross-cultural situation. He already knew the people, the country and the culture of Rhodesia, and had learned the dialect of the people as a young child. Seeing the joy and enthusiasm that his parents had in serving Christ left him certain that there could be no more challenging or fulfilling career for him than to return to the mission field. As is the experience of many missionary kids, he had to work through the question of whether he was returning to Africa just because it was his homeland. He wrestled with the answer to that by asking God to close the door if he was returning to Africa for the wrong reason. God confirmed Lynn's dream, and he began preparatory studies at Northeastern Bible College.

***

Lynn and I dated for all four years of Bible college. When we were in our senior year, he was ready to ask my dad for permission for us to be married. Lynn was unsure of exactly how to do that. Our college was in New Jersey, and my dad lived in Long Island. But to make it more challenging, my dad was a tugboat captain. He worked away from home for two weeks at a time. When Lynn called my house, my mother told him that dad was away for another week. It was a custom to announce engagements at the college Christmas formal, just two weeks away, so the timing was awkward.

Lynn called our house to speak to my dad. He was away, so Lynn asked my mother if there was a way to contact him at work. My mother hesitated a little. Lynn explained why he was asking. He was in a bit of a time crunch and wanted to get permission from my dad soon, to fit all of the other pieces in place (like the actual proposal). My mother gave Lynn a number. As a family, we all knew that the number was used only for emergencies, but Lynn felt that this was a pretty urgent matter.

My dad was definitely a man of few words, a deep thinker and not very chatty. Lynn rang through to my dad. "Hi Captain Sherman, this is Lynn." A silence followed. Lynn tried to make a light conversation to loosen Dad up. That not working, he cut to the chase. "Captain Sherman, you know that Judy and I have been dating for four years now." More silence from my dad. "I was wondering if I could have your blessing to ask Judy to marry me?" A little more silence (I was his only daughter, so maybe he was just contemplating?) "Captain Sherman, are you still there?" Finally, my dad responded. "I don't care what you do, Son, but just get off this line."

Lynn wasn't quite sure how to take my dad's response, but he hung up. Later, Lynn found out that he was talking to my father on ship-to-shore radio, which is why we only used that phone for absolute emergencies. Dad said that the call was heard by every ship and tugboat from Maine to Florida. For the rest of the day, he was getting calls, "Captain Sherman, can I please marry your daughter?"

We were married just a week after graduation. Our life together would turn out to be the story I dreamed of as a teen. Even when I didn't have a distinct plan for my life, God's finger prints were there all the time.

Lynn and Judy on their wedding day

2

Ellsworth

Who would ever have thought that a large, handmade paper mâché elephant could be such an incredible blessing in our lives? Yet an elephant made more than 50 years ago is still one of our most treasured memories.

We were living in New Jersey, expecting our first child and awaiting clearance from our sending organization for our first trip to Africa as missionaries, when we were contacted by a youth group from a church in Staten Island, NY. The church had been a financial and prayer supporter of Lynn's parents, also missionaries, for many years. Though the church itself was not planning to support us as missionaries; the youth of the church wanted to get involved in our ministry.

In February 1969, we were invited to speak to this group of high school students. We arrived at the church, excited to tell these teenagers about our upcoming trip. Shortly before we were introduced to speak, one of the teens ran into the room shouting, "Ellsworth is coming, Ellsworth is coming." It was an unusual announcement, but we were with high school kids, right? Just as Lynn started to speak, another teenager came running into the room: "Ellsworth is coming, Ellsworth is coming!"

We were baffled, but we managed to finish the presentation without any more Ellsworth warnings. However, before we returned to our seats, we had our answer. Several of the young people marched in with a very large paper mâché elephant. They told us that it had been made to be a bank. The students had taken on the challenge, on their own, of raising enough money to buy tickets for Lynn and me and our newborn to travel to Africa. The cost for three one-way airline tickets was $1150. Using bake sales, work days, washing windows and baby-sitting jobs, the young people had a plan to fill that big elephant bank with enough money to purchase our airline tickets.

Several months later, in April, we were invited back to speak at their church. Our daughter Kim was two weeks old at that time.

We discovered that the students had broken open the elephant bank that contained their earnings, and that day they presented us with a check for $1150. We were overwhelmed. Their thoughtfulness and love have been a reminder of God's goodness through the years of our ministry.

3

Preparing to Go

The June departure for Africa had finally come. I was 23 years old. We had a precious, two-month-old baby girl, Kimberly Joy. The dream of serving God in Africa that had been put on my heart and that I had committed my life to when I was 16 years old, was being fulfilled.

We drove to Long Island, New York, from our tiny, little garage apartment in New Jersey to spend our last weekend stateside with my parents. Kim was their first mutual grandchild. Mom was a Christ follower by this time, but my dad wasn't. We had decided to move 10,000 miles away to serve God, and we were taking their precious little granddaughter with us. Our terms of service overseas were five years long, so Kim would most likely be ready to go to kindergarten the next time they would see her.

Even knowing that, Mom seemed so happy for us. Unbeknownst to me, she was keeping a lot of stress and concern tucked inside. Those last hours before leaving for JFK airport were spent packing and saying good-bye to my family. My older brother said that he thought we were totally crazy. "There are many people in America that need to hear about God; why are you going so far across the world to do this?"

In my joy and enthusiasm for the adventure before us, I failed to notice how anxious Mom really was. She never said a word about the inner pain she was feeling about our going to a country so far away. She had heard of the Unilateral Independence and knew that there was much unrest in the country. When it was almost time for us to leave for the airport, Mom had not yet gotten out of bed. She was an early riser, so this was very curious.

I well remember the aching feeling in the pit of my stomach when I went into my mother's room. She was deathly pale with dark rings under her eyes. Mom then told me that my dad had just called an ambulance. She was having severe internal bleeding, and their doctor had advised that she go directly to the hospital. She did not want me to be concerned so she had not told me.

What a horrific quandary! Our flight was booked and we could not easily change it. Scores of people were planning to be at the JFK airport to see us off. But how could I leave my mother, not knowing what was really wrong? How serious it was? Would I ever see her again? Does God want us to go ahead with our plans? Mom strongly encouraged us to go on as scheduled. As I think back now, I don't believe that I could have been as gracious as Mom. "Judy, go ahead! God has opened all the doors for you; you need to go ahead."

All of us were crying. Dad looked at me with sadness. I was their love child. They lived together for nine years before marrying, which back in the 1940's was quite unusual. I had been his little princess from the day I was born, and now I was leaving them for five years, going into unknown territory, considered by many as *Deep, Dark Africa.*

From early in my life, Dad had faith in me. He convinced me that I could do whatever I set my mind to. My trips to Lower East Side New York as a lone 15-year-old girl, by bus and two subways, to teach in a small African American church every Sunday always had my parents' blessing. They were not Christ followers themselves when I was young, but they encouraged me to spread my wings. When I committed my life to Christ, the strength and the courage to do whatever God put in my path was made even easier because of the way my parents believed in me and encouraged me to step up to what was set before me. God Himself gave me peace. He gave me strength. Fear had never been a part of my growing up, so I was able to leave on this journey to Africa.

My dad's love for my mom was deep; their love for each other was an example to me of commitment. But now, Dad was naturally very worried about Mom and whatever illness was lying ahead for her. He never asked or urged me to stay back or falter in the course that was set before me. His encouragement made me love him more. Even though he was not a Christ follower, he understood our commitment and, in his own way, was very proud of the decision we had made.

If I close my eyes, I can still see the pain in Dad's eyes. He never questioned or said a word as we prayed with him and Mom and then took their precious grandbaby away. We headed to the airport as he and Mom awaited the ambulance. I can still feel the tearing in my heart, like it was literally being torn out of my chest. We went with their blessing, but I had imagined Mom and Dad by our sides at the airport waving us off, so the day seemed dimmer.

***

We got to the airport in time to check our suitcases and begin the goodbyes to all those dear folk who came to see us off: my three brothers and their families, former Sunday school teachers, close friends, and representatives from our supporting churches. There were also representatives from the church that had built Ellsworth. About 50 people were gathered there to send us off. We were very excited for the journey ahead of us, and yet my heart was aching at the farewell to my parents, wondering if I would ever see Mom again.

We truly had been assured by God that this was a journey that He was making with us. He was going to be in front of us and in back of us, every single step of the way. We boarded the plane and the tears subsided as we got nestled in the seats that would take us to Switzerland and then on to Africa. God's peace was like a warm blanket around us. He had promised peace when we committed to follow Him, and He had shown Himself faithful.

All of a sudden, I heard a very familiar voice and saw my dear college friend, Bette, running down the aisle of the airplane looking for me. Although Bette and I had been together in college only one year, we were soul mates and made so many memories together, sharing Jesus on the streets of New York and the beaches of Long Island. What was she doing on the plane?

Bette had convinced the flight attendants, who had already shut the jet doors, that she REALLY needed to say good bye to her best friend, and down the aisle she came until she found our seats. Bette had gotten caught in traffic coming all the way from Pennsylvania and had finally arrived at JFK, only to find that we had already boarded and the door was firmly shut. We hugged and laughed and promised to write all the time. The tears flowed again until she was safely off the plane. It was time to take a deep breath and settle down again. We were on our way!

Judy, Lynn and Kimberly headed to Africa

4

Cultural Learning

We arrived in what was then Rhodesia, in 1969. The government had declared its independence from England five years before. Salisbury was the capital at that time, and we spend our first few weeks there with Lynn's parents, Thelma and Norman, who had been missionaries there since 1946. Calls to and from the US were very rare and expensive, so I had not spoken to anyone about my mom while we were traveling to Africa. Through the crackles and echoes of a long-distance call, we learned that she had spent some days in the hospital, was stabilized from bleeding ulcers, and she was released to go home.

Kim was Thelma and Norman's first grandchild, and it was fun for them to get to know her. During the time with them, we shopped for furniture as we brought none with us. We awaited the arrival of the little truck that we had imported. What a blessing to have veteran missionaries like Lynn's parents to advise us on how to stock up on groceries and staples for our first three months—things we would need to live in the bush! When the truck arrived, we loaded it and headed out for Chironga Missions Station which was a three- to four-hour drive from Salisbury.

I knew the ride would be long; the road was paved for part of the way, but then the pavement suddenly stopped. We found ourselves on what seemed like endless corrugated packed dirt that made Lynn grip the steering wheel so hard that his knuckles turned white and his hands vibrated long after we reached our destination.

Since this was my first trip to the African bush, I was filled with anticipation. Because it was the dry season, we were frequently thirsty, and stopped often at the little stores along the way to get drinks. Remembering Lynn's story about his dad's early experience in the bush, I decided that I would slow down on my beverage drinking. Once while his dad was in their outhouse, a cobra came slithering up between his legs! He had the presence of mind to not make a move and just let the snake leave, which it did. I hoped that I would never, ever have to use an outhouse because there is no way that I would have sat so still!

After several hours of driving, we reached Mt. Darwin, the closest town to our destination. We still had more than an hour to drive to reach the mission station of Chironga.

At Chironga, we were welcomed by Marg and Russ Jackson, veteran missionaries, who would be our Shona language teachers. After a lovely dinner, we walked to what would be our first African home. To my delight, it had lovely indoor plumbing–no outhouse to be seen.

My goal for the next few months was to learn as much as I could about both the language and the culture of the Shona people. Lynn had grown up there, so he already knew and loved the people, but I was totally clueless. I was blessed to have Russ and Marg as our teachers because they not only knew the Shona language but also loved the culture.

Part of language school training was getting further into the rural areas, to spend weekends in different villages. Along with the Jacksons, we would pack our two trucks with enough gear, water and food for three days, then drive for several hours. After we set up camp, we would walk to visit the local people in their small mud, thatched-roof huts. We would listen to their stories, observe their culture, and talk with them.

In the Shona culture, one of the ways to show respect for an older person was to keep your head lower than theirs, either by staying seated or by curtseying. We learned their traditional greetings, and the importance of tea breaks at 10 and 3, daily. In that rural culture, respectable women wore skirts or dresses, with sleeves, and never pants.

When Sunday mornings dawned, we looked forward to having church services and then heading home. One very hot Sunday, when the temperature was well over 100 degrees, we had church in the local school. The beautiful, rich harmony of Shona singers, with drums to accompany them, opened our time of worship together. Church usually lasted several hours. Even the missionaries who spoke Shona best were usually followed by a recap from the Emcee, who repeated what was preached and gave a summation of the whole service.

To our surprise, immediately after church, the wife a teacher invited us to their home for lunch. She had cooked an amazing meal of Sadza and chicken. Sadza, the staple diet of the Shona people had become our favorite food. It was made of white corn meal, stirred into boiling water. Additional corn meal was added until the porridge had a very stiff consistency, so stiff that when you broke off a piece with your hands, and rolled it up into a ball, it left no corn meal mixture on your hands. We ate with great joy and felt no shame at how much we had consumed. We had overindulged for sure, but when she offered us a piece of chocolate cake, it looked too delicious to turn down! We left feeling like we had just eaten a huge Thanksgiving dinner.

It was time to leave in the heat of the day, and the thought of a cool shower and a cold Coke was great. We would then nap on our fairly cool cement floor, which we found to be the coolest place on a hot afternoon.

After saying goodbye to this dear teacher and his wife, we got in our two trucks and started home. We did not get far. A young girl was standing in the middle of the road, flagging us down. Russ, who was in the lead, stopped to talk to the girl.

"Mufundisi, Ambuya wangu, wakakubikira sadza." "Teacher (term of respect), my grandmother has cooked sadza for you."

It was now after midday and the heat was climbing. We had overindulged already and topped it off with chocolate cake! Baby Kim was ready to have a cool bath and sleep in her little cot.

But we did not want to offend this gracious village woman by refusing her kind invitation for lunch. So, off we went to follow this little girl. She was running ahead of our trucks to show us the way. There were no marked roads, and she wanted to show us where tree stumps and potholes were.

We arrived at Ambuya's (grandma's) village and were in for quite an afternoon. The dog and cats that we met as we got out of our truck were not in very good shape physically, and the dubious stage was set for our lunch date.

A village was compromised of 2-3 huts made from mud brick, each with a thatched roof made from long grass. There was typically a sleeping hut or two, usually with a small fire in the middle to keep them warm and a kitchen hut where the pots and pans were stored and the cooking was done inside if the weather was inclement. Sometimes there were benches made of mud around the circumference of the circular wall of the hut. We have been in some very beautiful huts, with ledges to display the cook ware and mud shelves to display their plates. A village typically belongs to only one family, which would include the parents and often the grandparents and any of the young children living there. As we stood at the edge of the village, we noticed that there were several huts. For proper village etiquette, one stands at to the edge of the outer "imaginary" ring around the circle of huts, and calls out, "Go go Goi" similar to our knocking at some one's house. You wait there, not entering the circle, until you are invited in. After the head of the home, or whoever happened to be the oldest and at home at the time, would reply "Pindai enyu," you would could go further into the village.

Typically, there would be a fire, found in the center of the circle of huts. When the weather was amenable, that was the gathering place. A bonde, a mat made of river reeds, was usually available on the ground near the fire and that would be where we would sit. Sometimes, there were log stumps or large rocks, available for men to sit as well. The little girl's grandma, Ambuya, came out to greet us. What a sweet thoughtful lady! She had heard that there were visitors in the area, and she went out of her way to host us. So many life lessons to be learned from these gracious rural people.

Making Sadza

Typical African Village

After the obligatory greetings of hand clapping and curtsying, which always start every conversation, she directed us to a small hut at the back side of the village. This was quite unusual for us not to sit with the family to eat, but in retrospect, it was a blessing that we were eating alone. In the hut there was a small wooden table and four chairs. The walls had recently been painted black and treated with the insecticide, DDT. This insecticide has an incredibly pungent oder--an overwhelming smell that can practically take your breath away. It had apparently been applied recently to disinfect and drive away any insects.

This second and quite unexpected lunch was being served at around 2 PM, at the pinnacle of heat for the day--probably 110-115 degrees and no ventilation. There was one tiny window, placed very high on the wall. The powerful smell of DDT in combination with the heat, created a feeling of malaise. Since we had just eaten about a half an hour before, we weren't the tiniest bit hungry.

Sadza, as I mentioned, is the main food served twice a day in every Shona home. It was for sure one of our favorites. But the meal sticks to your ribs for hours and hours! It is best served piping hot. This precious grandmother must have cooked the sadza that she was serving us very early in the day. It had hardened with a stiff crust on the top. It was cold and almost impossible to penetrate. The second dish was okra. Boiled okra is delicious when served hot—this was not. We tried breaking off chunks of hardened sadza and dipping into the okra, but the cold, slimy okra just slipped off the cold sadza.

Russ wanted us to learn the culture--what was appropriate and what was inappropriate. Certainly, for a meal so lovingly prepared, it would be inappropriate to leave it untouched. But Russ found this particular situation quite puzzling; he was at a loss to decide how best to handle it. There was no way, with how full we were and how cold the food was, that we could eat this meal, however graciously it was prepared. But Russ knew we had to at least make a dent in it, Fortunately, one of the "cultural rules" was that you never were expected to eat all the food that was set before you. If you did, it would indicate to the hostess that you actually could have eaten more, and she would assume that she had not provided a sufficient amount. Knowing that little nugget was a blessing.

Russ was pondering his options! How could we at least make a dent in the abundance of food that had been set before us? Lynn and I could not think of any suggestions to make. Russ looked up at the single small window. Could we throw some of the sadza out of the window and feed the obviously under-nourished dogs and cats? No, that would not work. Even if we stood on the chair, the window was way too high!

"Marg, do you have a purse with you?"

"No, I left it in the truck," replied Marg.

"Judy, do you have a diaper bag?'

"No, I left it in our truck."

"Ok; let's review the options are left to us so that we don't appear rude."

After a few minutes, Russ stood up with a look of victory and accomplishment. We watched in amazement as Russ broke off chunks of the cold sadza and filled his pants pockets with it. He felt that he had found the solution. There was still enough sadza and okra left in the bowls so that Ambuya would feel that she had given us enough to eat.

The four of us adults and baby Kim, who had been quite a star through this whole day of heat and no naps, slipped out of the hut to say goodbye to our gracious host. In our years of serving in Africa, I have found that there is no way to outgive an African hostess. The Shona people are so kind and giving. Outside, Ambuya asked if we would say a prayer to bless her village. "Of course," said Russ, "we would be honored to do that." As was the custom, we all knelt down at the center of the village to pray. Just before Russ started to pray, Ambuya called out to her little granddaughter, the one who had directed us to her village. "Musicana (little girl), while we are praying, please would you catch that rooster?" And she pointed to the big red rooster that had been proudly strutting around the village.

We were kneeling in the dirt, and I was attempting to follow the prayer in Shona, but it was hard not to giggle with the sounds of this little girl chasing the rooster around the circle of kneeling people. Imagine the sound of this rooster being chased, NOT wanting to be caught and objecting LOUDLY!!

But who was the final winner? The little girl! She caught the rooster and tied his feet together with some bark stripped off a tree. That rooster was not planning to go quietly; he continued his protests with LOUD cock-a-doodle-doos! I can't remember a word of what Russ prayed in that benediction, but I can certainly tell you the sound of that protesting rooster. All the while, Russ, still praying, was also attempting to shoo away the hungry dogs and cats that had discovered a treasure--two pockets full of sadza.

As we were ready to go, Ambuya ceremoniously presented the rooster to Marg. She held it tightly, trying to avoid being pecked as he continued to loudly protest.

After we thanked her for the hospitality, we started to walk to our two trucks. All was going well, with Ambuya, the little girl, and her brothers following behind us closely to wave us off. All of a sudden it dawned on Russ! The keys for the truck! They were stuffed, down deep in his pockets, under fistfuls of sadza and cold okra.

Marg, Lynn and I tried to suppress our giggles and kept chatting with Ambuya, while Russ gave notice that he needed to use the outhouse.

Learning the Culture–an important part of the foundation for our 14 + year stay in Zimbabwe. This was not as new to Lynn, but for me, it was very different from my New York culture. Fortunately, we were being taught by an amazing couple who had lived in the country for decades and who genuinely loved and valued the culture of the Shona people. We learned more by spending our weekends camping with the people than sitting all day with books. The foundation built in those months forged in us such a deep love for the Shona people that it is with us until this day. Each experience was a building block that God used to create deep and loving relationships.

5

So Much to Learn

There were so many adjustments for me, the girl from New York City, when we arrived at Chironga Station in July, 1969. In many ways, the confidence that my parents built in me was such a help in this new adventure. But I very quickly realized that my real confidence was not in myself, but rather in trusting God for each of the new things that we were facing. He was the One who was my strength and only He gave me true confidence.

One of many things that we learned from Thelma, Lynn's mom, was about the water in Africa. The water we used at the house was pumped up from the river. The river water was filled with a parasite called bilharzia. As a result, all the water that we used for bathing, cooking, and cleaning dishes had to be treated and boiled. Handling the water situation was a huge learning curve for me.

Lynn was going to be away one afternoon, and he asked me to tend to the water in the 44-gallon steel drum. The drum was nestled into a three-sided brick fireplace and after we filled it with water, we would make a fire under it. The plan was to bring the water to a boil and let it boil for about 20 minutes, which would kill germs and the parasites. However, we should not let it boil longer because too much water would boil away. Off went Lynn,

Our water heater

and I was the over-confident little newbie to Africa who thought for sure I could manage just boiling water.

I could –until the 20 minutes was up. Lynn didn't tell me how I was supposed to "turn off" the fire and stop the water from boiling away. I started by pulling out a few logs to slow the rolling boil, but the white-hot coals enclosed in that three-sided fireplace were keeping the water very hot. What was I to do? I didn't know how to stop the boiling. What would I have done with a fire in New York? Water! I would extinguish the fire with water. I quickly ran and got a bucket of water and tossed it onto the fire. Immediately I realized that was a very bad idea. From the three-sided brick enclosure, the red-hot ash had nowhere to go except out the front, where I was standing. And out it came, exploding all the steam, coals and ash in a big burst over my hands!

After running to get Kim from her nanny Orpah, I raced to Marg's house and cried out in pain, "What should I do? What can I do?" In those days it was thought that butter would heal all burns, so we covered my hands with butter and wrapped them. The burning became even more intense, as the butter actually sealed the burn and made it worse.

We decided I should drive to our mission hospital while Marg kept Kim. I jumped into our little Isuzu Wasp truck. The drive to the hospital was not that long, only about seven miles, but with the potholes and curves, the intense burning in my hands, and waiting for herds of cows or goats to clear the road made it seem like an eternity. I could hardly see for the tears of pain streaming down my face, but I finally made it to that wonderful sign, Karanda Hospital.

I parked and went in to find a doctor. The doctors and nurses at that rural hospital were some of the most dedicated people that I have ever met, dealing regularly with situations much more severe than my burned hands. Their work was more than just a job; it was their passion, and they did it faithfully for God. Doctor Roland Stephens, who later did amazing surgeries on war casualties, told me that I had second-degree burns. He cut off my engagement and wedding rings and peeled off the dead skin before applying burn ointments and wrapping my wounds.

I drove home rejoicing in both Dr. Roland Stephens's knowledge and in the tender care of my heavenly Father. I had so much to learn in this new country, but I was thankful for an amazing God who walked with me day by day.

Judy with bandaged hands

6

Encounter With My First Snake

I have never loved snakes. Nor eels, worms, or anything that wiggles. The unpleasant memory started, I think, when my parents came home one night carrying a bag of live eels. Dad put the eels in the kitchen sink full of water, and let them swim around. He was quite excited to share with me that you can put a live eel in the freezer and when they thawed, they would revive. Dad thought that it would be a really good idea for me to pick them up. I was not as enthusiastic as my dad. I was his princess. He rarely scolded me, even the many times I am sure that I needed it. He never spanked me! But that night, he was determined that I should lift up these two eels. I politely declined. Dad insisted. I declined a little stronger. Dad wanted to show me that there was no harm that would come to come to me from these eels, and he wanted my mom to show me how easy and safe it was. "Mom, pick up the eel and show Judy that she won't get hurt." My dear mother was very compliant and proceeded to pick up an eel in each hand. Those eels just did their wiggle, wiggle thing and scared the life out of me. I did not want to hold those slippery creatures.

Pursuing his plan, Dad said, "Judy, pick up the eels. Your mom did it and she is fine." Unwisely, I again refused! I think it was one of the only times my dad felt I was deserving of a strong reckoning–and I was punished for it. He was very respectful of my mom, and he felt that my refusal was disrespecting her. Needless to say, from that day on, snakes, eels, worms –anything that wiggled like that–were not my friends.

***

In Africa, encounters with snakes were my main concern. On the way to Chironga, I recollected my father-in-law's experience with a cobra in the outhouse. I was soon to hear many more stories of people's encounters with snakes. What an amazing comfort to know that one of the earliest directors of our mission, TJ Bach, had prayed years before that no TEAM missionary would ever be bitten by a snake. To this day, that has held true. However, there have been many very close encounters.

Still in language school, I was sitting inside our home, studying my Shona lessons, when Lynn came into the house. He went to the locked gun case, and I could hear him opening it and removing his shotgun. I followed him out and saw a poisonous puff adder sitting by our back porch. It was close to coming to our veranda where Orpah and Kim were playing. Lynn was able to shoot him before he harmed any of us. Happy for me...one less menacing creature.

The very next day, Lynn walked up to the table where I was studying, again with a shotgun in hand. Then he said, "Judy, please come outside with me." I was very curious. Cobras are one type of the many poisonous snakes that are found in Africa, probably next in line to black or green mambas. When frightened or ready to attack, cobras raise up their head and sit up hooded, poised, ready to strike. Even though we had lived in Africa only a few weeks, Lynn felt that it would be good for me to face my fears and shoot this poisonous guy. The cobra was still hooded and upright as we approached him, right outside our house.

It was the first time I had ever even held a gun in my life.

"Where do I aim?" I asked Lynn.

"Try to get him in the head!" he said.

The snake was about five feet away just outside our gate. I aimed at the intruder's head. He did not stay still while I took time to steady the heavy shotgun on my shoulder; he kept moving from side to side. I aimed and fired.

Besides knocking my shoulder to kingdom come, I was delighted that I got him in what I considered the neck. Cobras are known for being able to spit with accuracy even after being decapitated. He was still wiggling around when Lynn took another shot and finished him. The very present danger was taken care of. My shoulder really hurt after the kick of the shotgun. We walked back into the house to be met by a very large scorpion in the kitchen. Lynn killed it. I realized that my introduction to African life was happening very quickly. I had had enough wild life for one day, thank you. I was very thankful for God's protection. He had given me an awesome respect for the creatures that could do harm.

Did I conquer my dislike of those wiggly creatures? Not really. To this day, I let my grandkids put worms on the hook when we go fishing! God saw a need for snakes, worms, and scorpions, but I don't. I can do without them in or near my home, no matter where I live.

7

Behind the Wheel

I grew up in Bellerose, Long Island, one of the suburbs of New York City, and our family didn't own car. My parents always felt that it was much more convenient to use public transportation. That was true at least with my dad's job as a tugboat captain. Dad had to travel to work only once every two weeks, and then he stayed on the boat for 14 days before coming home for a week. He felt there was no need to have a car sitting at our house.

When we needed to travel, we walked 3/4 of a mile to the bus station; took the Q36 bus to Jamaica; transferred to the F subway to get to downtown Manhattan; and then transferred to the E train to get to Brooklyn where all of our extended family lived. When the weather was good, it was easy. However, Christmas, New Year's, St Patrick's Day and a variety of christenings, confirmations and funerals that we attended, fell in the snowy, cold winter months. That was not quite as easy. Especially the coming home late part, traveling by the subways and walking the last stretch, after my parents did much "celebrating" with the Irish side of the family.

As a result, getting a driver's license was never on my radar. Lynn assured me that it was really hard to get a license in Rhodesia. He had tried a few times and failed before he finally got it.

At his urging, shortly before we were ready to leave for Africa, I realized that I had to bite the bullet and get my license. I did not do very well. Actually, I did terribly.

I was eight months pregnant when I signed up. My required three-point turn had at least six points. My parallel parking was less than spectacular–I was about five feet from the curb. I could hardly fit behind the wheel and reach the pedals because of my very pregnant, very big belly.

During the test, I had a really good chat with the examiner. I told him that as soon as I had the baby, which was decidedly imminent, we were going to head out to Africa.

"With a brand new baby?" he asked rather incredulously.

Nervous perspiration dripped down my face and back as I very poorly executed his instructions. However, my baby news seemed to make him forget my poor driving skills. He was a Catholic man, and his wife was also having their first baby the following month. The coincidence of it all must have touched his heart (and blurred his perception as a driving test examiner). It was a wonderful to be able to share with him why we were pulling up stakes and heading to Africa to share the love of Jesus with the people there.

As we finished the driving course, the examiner told me to pull up by the building and stop. I did. But I was about 20 yards short of where he wanted to be left off. I groaned, embarrassed when he asked me to restart the engine and pull up a little closer to the building.

I said, with much chagrin, "I guess I failed, didn't I?"

He said, "Well, I really should fail you, but I can tell that you are a woman of faith. If you promise to pray for my wife and a safe delivery for our baby, I will pass you, mainly because you are going to Africa, and all you can kill there are elephants."

I almost hugged him but decided to stop while I was ahead, so I agreed and thanked him.

***

I must admit that his words did come bouncing back one cold, dark August night when we were in language learning in Africa. We had moved to Chironga for our time of language and cultural training. A wonderful young man named Accordion was working for us part time. He worked so hard chopping wood and helping me around the house with chores that were new and unfamiliar to me...unlike things I did in New York. Accordion lived in a village a few miles from our house. Lynn usually would drive him back to his village after work. One night, Lynn was away, and I felt bad that Accordion had to walk home alone in the dark, so I offered to drive him. Accordion agreed. (Obviously, word from the driving school examiner had not reached him in rural Africa.) What could possibly go wrong on a three-mile drive? I dropped Kim off for what I thought would be a few minutes with our language teacher, Marg, and off we went.

The roads in rural Africa are very, very narrow. The one-lane road rose to a ridge in the middle, similar to a camel's hump. The sides of the road are quite sandy. There is definitely room for only one car at a time. When two cars met, one would have to pull off the road, onto the grass if there was any flat area nearby.

My experience as a driver was a total of five months. Our little Blue Isuzu 4-cylinder Wasp truck was a stick shift diesel. Driving stick shift had been a new experience for me. Our diesel truck also did not have very much UMPH! I learned that if we were at the bottom of a steep hill, the little truck usually did not have enough power to make it to the top of the hill. One of us (it was usually me since Lynn was the better driver) had to get out and push it to get it up the hill.

Accordion and I chatted on the way to his village, each with very limited knowledge of the other's mother tongue. I dropped him off at a place in the road near his village and then had to do a U-turn to get back in the direction of my home. I remembered that 6-point turn from my driving exam. With no power steering in the truck and the verges of the road surrounded by piles of sand, I was doing at least six points for my three-point U-turn. At one of the many points, I backed into the sandy bank in the ditch. Try as I may, I got the hitch and the back of the truck stuck deeper and deeper into the dirt.

Now what should I do? There were no cell phones, no corner gas stations, and Accordion was already safely into his village. No one could be seen in any direction. I walked off the road towards Accordion's village. It was pitch black. Have I mentioned how dark the African sky is at night? Or how brilliant the stars were, looking like diamonds on a black velvet cloth? Did I mention that this was two days after my encounter with two poisonous snakes that were right by our back door? Oh, if only it were 35 years later, and I had a cell phone! But alas, I did not.

Some of Accordion's family members must have heard my truck screeching and spinning wheels trying to get out of the sand trap. They met me and valiantly attempted to get my truck unstuck, but to no avail. I sat by the side of the road near their village for what felt like half of a lifetime on that still, dark, starry night. I recited all the verses I knew about God being with me.

Psalm 46:10 came to mind: *"Be still and know that I am God."* I was still, for sure! I will admit, there were a few times when my mind was telling me that the whole family of the cobra that I had killed the day before was coming looking for me. But surprisingly, what I felt the most was peace–an amazing peace, considering where I was sitting.

Another verse came to me, and I played and replayed it in my mind. Psalm 46:1 says, *"GOD IS OUR REFUGE AND STRENGTH, ALWAYS READY TO HELP IN TIMES OF TROUBLE."* I felt HIS presence like a blanket wrapped around me; He was there with me.

Sitting there, alone in the dark, I heard the sound of what I was sure was a white horse, galloping in my direction to rescue the damsel in distress (Ok, it was the sound of a motorbike; Lynn and Uncle Russ were coming to find me). They were such a welcomed sight and with a little help from our friends in Accordion's village, we successfully extricated our little truck from its resting place. Needless to say, Lynn drove me home. We collected Kim then rested well, safe in our bed.

As I reflect on that night, the most meaningful part was experiencing God's promise that He would always be there, right by my side, no matter how dark the night. Trucks–not so much, but God is faithful.

Neighbors from local villages always willing to help

8

The Fire Walkers

One morning during language school, we heard quite a bit of commotion in the valley down below our house. Lynn was curious as to what was going on and hopped on his motorbike to do some investigating. What he found was a large gathering of white-robed men, women and teenagers building a large fire pit, around 12 feet long, six feet wide and about two feet deep.

He found out that the group was known as the Vaapostori (The Apostles). They were planning to have a large district meeting there in the valley. Having just started a fire in the trench, their plan was to add logs all day so they would have a large bed of red-hot coals by their evening service. Lynn started a conversation with the leaders and found out quite a bit about their plans. They asked if Lynn would be willing to preach at the meeting. Lynn declined preaching, but he asked if he could come back for the service and bring others. Later that evening, we could see the huge fire burning much brighter than earlier in the day.

As evening settled into the dark, starry night, we heard lovely singing that was loud and rich. The harmony of a hundred or so African voices filled the air and echoed beautifully through the valley. True to his word, Lynn took Marg, Russ and me to the service. It was an impressive sight: over a hundred people in their long white robes, singing with great enthusiasm.

The Vaapostori are a sect that has a very large following among rural African people. Back in 1914, a man named Johane Masowe was born in South Africa. He grew up to be a preacher and said that he had a personal vision of God. He believed that he, personally, was the reincarnation of John the Baptist, who lived during the time of Jesus Christ. His following continued to grow and today is one of the largest religious sects in Africa.

That night, we found ourselves in the midst of this large group of people who were singing and chanting. They began working themselves into a frenzy. The leader of the group came over to where we were sitting and again asked if Lynn or Uncle Russ would like to speak to the group. They both declined. Besides the beautiful singing, there seemed to be only chaos. There was a frenetic buzz in the air. As their chanting carried on, it became louder and louder. "UYA MWEYA, UYA MWEYA" (Come spirit, come spirit), and the frenzy increased. It was sad that they were not calling for the Holy Spirit (UYA MWEYA MUTSVENE) but just opened themselves up to whatever spirits were out there. The pit around which we were sitting was the focus of attention. The fire that we had seen from the top of the hill was now simmering down, and mainly white, hot coals remained.

I was mostly uncomfortable and somewhat fearful. I did not feel that we were in the presence of a Holy God, or that we were there to worship Him. We felt an uneasiness in our hearts. The oppression was like a wet, smothering blanket coming down over us; it even felt hard to breathe. The chanting grew louder and louder. Soon, a young girl in a long white dress, with her eyes closed and her arms crossed over her chest, started walking into the fire pit. She stumbled a little on the coals at first but then continued walking the length of the pit. She walked as if she were in a trance to the end of the 12-foot-long fire pit, back and forth, over and over again. Next, an older woman entered the pit and roamed back and forth over the coals, never flinching, with her white robe dragging into the hot coals but never set on fire. A man came close to us, bent over, picked up a handful of coals, and held them up to heaven without a murmur. One man, who had been trying to work himself up into the same frenzy as the rest of crowd, took one step onto the coals and screamed in pain. He obviously did not have the spirit that they were calling on. We watched several more people randomly walking in and out of the fire, almost like they were stepping into a pool of cool water, as the loud chanting continued and echoed through the valley.

Firewalkers on hot coals

It was unpleasant. It was scary. It was abnormal. It was oppressive. We felt like we were in the presence of an evil spirit. They called on powers and did things that were humanly abnormal. People were passing behind and around us, walking on the hot coals, while the chanters cheered them on. It seemed chaotic and out of control. We finally decided to leave, feeling shaken. We went back to our home, debriefed together about our experiences, and spent some time in prayer. We all expressed how thankful we were that we worshiped and served a God of order and of peace and not one of chaos.

***

Sadly, on each visit that we have made back to Africa in the past years, we have seen that this sect continues to grow. Their supernatural powers are drawing large followings. The pastors travel from village to village and expect to be treated with great superiority. They practice polygamy. They feel free to take wives from local villages whenever and wherever they stop to preach without being bound to the customary lobola (the bride price that is expected in the African culture) There is widespread abuse as they insist on taking girls twelve to fourteen years of age as their wives and then move on to another area to do the same. There are many branches of this group and each group seems to make up their own rules and interpretation of the Old Testament.

In the Bible, the Apostle John warns Christ followers to beware of False Teachers. That night, 51 years ago, we saw powerful false teachers attempting to bring new people into their fold. We are convicted that more needs to be done to teach the Living God to Africans who now succumb to superstition and the supernatural. We are told to "test the spirits to see whether they are from God," as "There are many deceivers who do not acknowledge Jesus Christ...in the world." The innocent people in the rural areas are being preyed upon. May God send His Word and His people to combat the evil.

9

First Thanksgiving in Africa

Thanksgiving was always a very special family time for my family. We were scattered in different states, but we always came together for Thanksgiving at my parents' home. My dad was a wonderful cook, and the turkey, of course, was the centerpiece. On Thanksgiving it was great to wake up to the smell of that turkey cooking. Since our move to Africa, I had not had a moment of homesickness, but I knew that it might be a little hard on me that first year, thinking of my extended family together. Of course, Thanksgiving is not a holiday that is celebrated in Africa. Phones, internet, and texting were not available, so I could not even call to talk to them.

Our final language exam almost coincided with Thanksgiving. I asked Lynn if we could drive to the closest town, Mount Darwin, to try to find a turkey. We could make the day one of "thanks for hopefully passing our exam." Lynn agreed. I went to the butcher and asked him if he had a turkey.

"Yes, we raise them for Christmas," he replied.

"Would there be any ready the last week of November?" I asked hopefully.

He said it was an unusual request, but he thought that he could find one that would be ready by then. I was elated. We could have our own small celebration, and maybe it wouldn't matter that 20 of my family members would not be present.

A few weeks later we made another trip to the butcher to pick up the turkey. He happily gave me a plump wonderful-looking turkey, and he also handed me the bill. Zimbabwe was still using British sterling as currency, and when I saw the price was £15, I almost choked. That was equivalent to $45 US. In 1969, that was an exorbitant amount of money for a turkey. I wrote out the check for him, and I am sure more than one tear dripped down on it. I carried the turkey outside and waited for Lynn to pick me up. I am sure he was assuming that I would be ecstatic with my purchase. Instead, when I got in the truck, I burst out in tears. Lynn asked what was wrong.

"I just paid $45 for a turkey," I replied. There was a dear group of widow ladies who lived in Brooklyn, New York who supported us with a combined gift of $15 every month. The cost of that turkey was three months' support from those ladies who gave sacrificially to support our ministry in Africa. I knew if I ate something that expensive, I would be thinking of them with every mouthful.

I looked at Lynn with my very soulful, teary eyes. "Please would you take this back in to the butcher and ask him if he would let us return it?"

Lynn was and is the most wonderful husband. He looked at my pathetic, crumpled face and agreed to try to return the turkey. He walked out of the butcher a few minutes later, a triumphant smile on his face. "Turkey returned." What a kind man! I am blessed. But it was a lesson I learned and God reminded me of often in the years ahead about who were really the ones sacrificing, and it was the ladies in Brooklyn.

***

A few days later was our language school final exam. I had worked so hard, but for Lynn, who spoke the language as a boy, it was a refresher course. The end result: I got two points higher on the final than Lynn. That was so fun and such a big accomplishment. In reality, I could pretty much only say "Good morning" or "Good Afternoon" or "How are you?" while Lynn could converse endlessly with anyone he met, and he could preach in Shona.

I smile thinking back on that learning experience. God is patient with us. He is kind, and He goes out of His way to teach us.

We found a chicken that one of our neighbors was willing to sell us and had an absolutely wonderful Thanksgiving, very appreciative of all that the Father had done for us in getting us ready for our next assignment. Those five months of learning language and culture, and even more importantly, the lessons of what we were truly thankful for, were foundational to the next 14 years of being in Zimbabwe.

10

Daily Life in Kapfundi

Looking back, 1969 was quite a year. Having a new baby in April, moving to Africa in June, God walking me through a huge learning curve to build the foundation for the next years of service, finishing language school, and getting our first assignment. We would be moving to the other side of the country. Lynn would become the manager of six local schools (something he never wanted to do, by the way). We were truly there, serving in Africa. Our joy was full to overflowing.

We were assigned by our mission board to move to Kapfundi Mission. It was at that time home to a local school for the children of the district as well as a clinic serving hundreds in the area.

Years before, Lynn's dad, Norman, had started a Bible School with six men under a tree in the Zambesi Valley. As the Bible School grew with more students, they moved to a few different areas, and Kapfundi was one of those places. It was a four to five-hour drive from the capitol city, Salisbury.

Lynn's father, in the 1950's, had built the home that we would be moving into. It was very nostalgic for Lynn to move back into his family home after all these years. Their family had loved that home and had such fond memories. Lynn and his brother attended boarding school when they were younger, but all of their school holidays were spent in that happy home.

The house was built from "ant hill dirt." Ant hills are red mounds, sometimes five to six feet tall. The red color comes from the excretion of white ants or termites. Those big red hills are dotted all over the rural African landscape. When the dirt is being used for building, it is shaped into bricks that are fired in a big kiln.

We did not have electricity for the seven years we lived there. Our refrigerator was run on paraffin gas; it needed to be filled every few days. The stove was bottled propane gas. Oil lamps and candles provided the light for our use in the evening. The big generator worked occasionally but seemed to be almost more trouble than it was worth to keep it running in the evening hours. It was constantly breaking down. But we were warm by the fire and cozy by lamp light every night.

Washing clothes was quite a long process. During our seven-year stay, we had two wonderful young women to help in the process that usually took two to three hours. The washing machine engine was from a lawn mower. However, the noisy, headache-inducing sound was so much better than the alternative of washing everything by hand as we had done in language school. Clothes were fairly easy, but jeans, sheets and towels were cumbersome.

The engine started with a pull cord. It had a wringer. We filled the machine with water and soap. The cleanest clothes went in first. After it agitated for a while, we would transfer the clothes from the machine into a cement basin of clean rinse water and scrub them to get out as much soap as possible. In the meantime, we put the next pile of clothes into the machine. The clothes continued to be transferred from machine to the cement tubs of water twice and then finally rinsed and put through the wringer one more time before being carried to the clothes line. Today, my wrinkled old hands and knuckles show the effects of the many times I got my hands stuck in the wringer as I urged the long sheets and towels through.

On warm sunny days, the process was easier because the clothes and sheets and towels dried quickly in the hot African sun. They smelled delicious after being hung on the line and air dried. Of course, having gone through the wringer three times, everything was pretty wrinkled. More often than not, buttons popped off as clothes were squeezed and rinsed. At the end, after washing the jeans and dark clothes, the water was emptied out on to the vegetables in the garden or on the fruit trees. What was left could be used to water the flowers that beautified the dusty landscape through the six months of the dry season, April-October.

The rainy season, of course, presented a bigger challenge; downpours occurred frequently. When we heard the sound of rain on our tin roofs, we would remember the clothes, and it was all-hands-on deck to get them in before they were soaked. Then we would wait for sunshine to appear again. When it didn't appear, we would drape the laundry over all of the furniture around the house. We went through this process twice a week, in the sun or rain.

The next part of the laundry process was a bit more challenging. After the clothes were dry and brought in off the line, every single piece had to be ironed. There is a fly in Africa, known as the Putsi Fly. While the clothes are on the line, the flies would lay their eggs on them. It was a problem when the clothes were put on, or diapers put on babies, or sheets were slept on. If the eggs were not killed through the ironing process, they would hatch and burrow under skin and little maggots were born. Thus, the ironing was important.

Since we did not have electricity, we came up with several fixes. One was a flat iron left on the coals of a burning fire. The iron would heat up enough to iron the clothes. I was blessed that there was always someone looking for work. I needed help to iron every piece of cleaned, dried laundry.

Another kind of iron opened on the top and could be filled with burning coals. This one was much more convenient in some ways because the coals stayed hot longer. But there was a downside too! Have you ever sat around a fire, making s'mores or just enjoying the dancing flames with coals popping, sending out sparks? That often happened when we were ironing. Most of our clothes were dotted with tiny burn marks from a spark landing them. Every sock, blouse, and pair of jeans; every towel, sheet, or anything that had been on the clothes line had to be ironed.

***

Although Africa has many amazingly beautiful flowers, animals, and fruits that we enjoyed immensely; there were also a few insects, bugs, and creatures that I might just need to chat with God about someday. One was the parasite called Bilharzia that lived on the edges of rivers and lakes. If we walked in, swam in, or played in one of those rivers or lakes on hot days, or drank the untreated water, the result was often Bilharzia. The host of the disease is a small snail that lives on the banks of rivers. If not wiped off quickly, the parasite burrows into the skin and settles into some organ of the body.

I could never thank the Lord enough for the wisdom and great advice that was passed on by my mother-in-law Thelma. She and Norman had been pioneer missionaries, arriving in what was then Rhodesia in 1946. Living their every-day life was so much harder than anything we ever experienced. Lynn's mom lovingly passed on many tips that kept us from getting Malaria, sleeping sickness, or Bilharzia. None of our family ever experienced the pain of a Putsi Fly maggot burrowed under our skin. There are so many other things that I learned from Lynn's mom and dad, and I was ever so thankful that I did not have to learn them from experience. We were incredibly healthy and happy all the years we lived in Zimbabwe.

***

One of the highlights of our time at Kapfundi was the birth of our first son, Rick. What a delight Rick was to us and a blessing to others around us. He was then and continues to be such a blessing in our lives. Our children were an incredible asset to our ministry. Family is extremely important in the Shona culture, and Kim and Rick opened the doors to friendship and ministry.

Shortly after his birth, we were asked to move temporarily to Salisbury to be house parents for one term at the children's hostel. It was a place for the children of missionaries in remote areas to live while they went to school in the city. Lynn and his brother had spent their early years there. The children ranged in age from 7-17. They missed their families, and would go home after each three-month term to spend three weeks. The second thing Lynn had not wanted to do, we did.

***

A favorite "God hug" came through soccer. Lynn had been a soccer player from his youth and still is to this day. Soccer became a way to connect with the local young men. Lynn was asked to play on their team, and they traveled weekly to games in the district. Our Saturdays would usually find the four of us getting on Lynn's motorbike and traveling to games. Or we might load the whole team into our truck to go to the game. Our two kids, with their blond cornsilk hair, were often the center of attention as we cheered for the Green Bombers, Lynn's team. Their sponsor was a local store keeper, Mr. Mudengazerwa. Knowing him opened a door of ministry for Lynn. Their friendship bonded through soccer.

We were on the mission station with a nurse, Lorraine. Without electricity or many modern things other hospitals and clinics had, Lorraine had to improvise in unbelievable ways. When babies were born prematurely, with no incubators available, she would get a small cardboard box, put a hot water bottle in it, and load it with small cotton balls. She would sit up all night, teaching the new mom how to use a syringe filled with breast milk to feed her little one. So many two- or three- pound babies would have died if not for Lorraine. She invested in all the local people, but she invested in our daughter as well.

Kim and Lorraine would walk hand in hand up the dirt road to our little clinic. She taught Kim how to help give care and was patient and loving as she worked with Kim. We loved our days at Kapfundi, and were blessed building friendships that exist to this day.

Learning to carry Kim like the local ladies did

God has a sense of humor. There were three things that Lynn never wanted to do: manage schools, parent in the mission kids' hostel, and work with English-speaking people. Two of three he had to do during our time at Kapfundi. However, it did not take much reflection to know that each of these things were building blocks of experience. Adventures at Kapfundi seemed to keep us on our toes and totally dependent on God. The days were sweet and most passed by with joy. We absolutely loved where God had us serving.

***

One weekend we found out that our friend Mr. Mudengazer-wa had been killed by those fighting the War of Independence. Two of his wives had also been killed. Shortly after that, a large missions station lost several missionaries, also from an attack by those being given weapons from outside countries. The roads were becoming more dangerous with landmines and attacks. Our leadership team decided that it was no longer safe for us to be in such an isolated area, and we were asked to move Bindura, a small farming and mining town on the other side of the country.

This move, however, would mean taking responsibility for a new group of English-speaking farmers and miners. His heart was with the Shona people and working with English-speaking Caucasians was another on the list of things that Lynn would prefer not to do. The decision to move took quite a bit of praying and discussion between us. Finally, the decision made, we were ready to move. I was seven months pregnant with our third child. God had new adventures planned for trusting Him and more unrevealed mysteries than we could have imagined. We were off to Bindura!

Visiting with an adorable village baby

11

Settling in Bindura

We loved our time in Kapfundi. We had learned so much about village life during our time at language school, and it carried over to our ministry. God had built a foundation that prepared us. We shared the love of God and stories from the Bible and had the privilege of starting new churches in some surrounding areas. We were thrilled to be serving God there. When we were approached by the Field Chairman and asked if we would consider moving to the town of Bindura, a small mining and farming town on the north east of the country, it was a hard decision for us. It was that third thing on Lynn's list of "I hope that I never am asked to do that."

Bindura was quite different from Chironga or Kapfundi. We had been pretty isolated in those two places for our first seven years. We changed from living in a small mud-brick home with no electricity to a bigger brick home with electricity. The water in the town of Bindura was treated and clean—not from a muddy river. And many of the people were English-speaking. We felt almost like we were back in the United States.

At our new home, flowers had been planted and the yard was beautiful. Russ, who had been living in the house before us, was a gifted gardener. More importantly, Marg and Russ had other gifts that fit into the ministry there. They were evangelists, and their work with a Bible study in their home had grown into a small church. Interestingly, we did not share their gifts, either in the garden or the ministry. They had no kids; they were free to come and go and visit people whenever they wanted. Our spiritual gifts were very different. Building relationships and discipleship was more our style. We had two children and were pregnant with our third child, which limited our mobility. However, when we arrived there, we thought we needed to be exactly like Marg and Russ. Looking back, we might have wasted much of our first two months trying to be them. We finally realized that if God wanted someone to be exactly like our predecessors, He could have just let them stay.

***

We settled quickly into life in Bindura. Kim and Rick started school, and they both got involved quickly in sports and activities of all sorts. Brad was born in the local hospital three months after we arrived and our lives definitely had a new rhythm. He became part of the fellowship that we were serving.

The church was growing and so they started using the local Dutch Reformed Church at alternate times when it was not being occupied. There were many more ladies than men in the church, and we were looking for opportunities to meet some of the younger men. We were thirty years old with three young children, and that opened doors to meet people. I joined the PTA, and we loved sports. Rugby was the sport of the town. Lynn had played rugby as a school boy. One week he headed to the rugby field, started playing, and soon he was accepted on the team. Before too long, one or two of the guys from the team started coming to church.

The war of independence in the mid-70's was a turbulent time. The country was continually on high alert as landmines were being detonated more frequently when cars passed over them on the roads. There were roadside attacks or direct attacks on people's homes. The road attacks often happened at dusk, and it was hard to do any tracking of the attackers as they escaped into the bush.

The government issued curfews all around the country. We were not to be on the roads between 4 PM and 6 AM.

Each Easter, we would have a sunrise service at a farm, but we had to go in convoy and have armed patrols accompanying us. Life was tense. Almost once a week, Lynn was doing the funeral of either a Shona brother or sister or someone in our English-speaking congregations. Each of our board members lost a member of their family during that time. One daughter died as her plane was shot down; one was killed by a landmine; and one, shot in an ambush on the road. Tension was mounting all over the country, and certainly in Bindura. All of the men were required to go on six-week stints protecting the area, which left wives and children home alone. However, it was time of spiritual growth as well. War time is not a time to sit on the fence when one is thinking about a relationship with God. It causes one to think of their mortality.

***

One weekend, during the rainy season, we had driven several hours to a new district. We crossed over some low-level bridges to get to Mushove. However, on our way home, after we packed up our tent in the rain and started the long drive, we arrived at a bridge where the water level had risen significantly; it was definitely too deep for us to cross. We parked the truck by the side of the road, gathered some firewood, and made a little fire to make tea as we waited until the water levels were low enough to cross the bridge. The water was raging over the bridge as it crossed over the concrete parapets and then rapidly rushed over the bridge and down the river with a huge gush.

Lynn would often put a big rock at the highest point to where the water had risen so that he could tell when the water was subsiding. This water was not subsiding. It was rushing so fast that it would have swept our truck down the river if we attempted to cross too soon.

We had our dog along with us, so while we waited for the river to go down, Lynn started throwing sticks into the water and watching the dog fetch the sticks and bring them back. They did this for quite a while, and two-year old Kim watched this playtime with giggles and great joy. Kim was into copying everything we did, and this time was no exception.

Lynn walked up the hill to where we had the chairs set up for tea. In a flash, Kim ran down to the bridge to the edge of the rushing river. She picked up a stick and threw it into the water like her dad had been doing with the dog. However, her throw went to the place where the whirlpools were deepest and spinning rapidly. She bent over to grab the stick as it was swirling back at her. In that second, Lynn saw her go for the stick and equally as quickly, watched her tumble head over heels into the raging whirlpool.

The water was muddy and swirling so fast that in that brief second, she was out of site. We had only a moment to react. In one quick swirl of the swift water, she would be over the ramparts and rushing down the river. Lynn literally had one chance to get her before she would be gone. As he was searching frantically, Lynn was begging God to let him find her. Then he saw it…her little white mop of hair sticking up like it had been electrified. With a burst of adrenaline and a strong sense of God's presence, he leaned in, grabbed her hair, pulled her out, and clutched her to his body. God allowed us to rescue our child. What a reminder of the sacrifice of our Heavenly Father who gave up His only child. With thankful hearts, we bundled her up and waited until the water subsided.

Lynn rescues Kim from the flooding river

12

Peace in Peril

Someone once asked me about our days in the country of Rhodesia, before it became Zimbabwe during the war for independence. They often asked, "What was your most memorable encounter with God during those years?" Through the 14 years that we lived there, our lives were punctuated many times with a need for total dependence on God. It is difficult to pick out only one that would characterize our relationship with God.

Lynn's childhood fluency in Shona, the dialect of the Chizizuru people, rapidly returned, and within months he was able to minister in a variety of ways, including managing six rural African school. The language came to me with ease. The Shona people are friendly and kind, so as I cooked with, sewed with, and made friends with the African women, I learned to speak their heart language.

We were living in the country when the war of liberation began to intensify. Land mines and attacks on buses and shots fired along the side of the road were becoming more frequent. There was now a real danger for our family to stay where we were, and it was decided by our leadership that we would move to a town and accept a new responsibility. With a certain amount of apprehension, we began a pastoral ministry in a small town across the country from where we had been living, nestled among some rolling hills. In addition to the privilege of pastoring that small gathering, part of our responsibility was church-planting and outreach ministry in the farm and mine compounds where hundreds of Africans were gathered for work opportunities. There were many English-speaking, white folk in the town who had been farming for several generations, as well as the many who were doing mining on the nickel mines. Lynn was used to working with the Shona-speaking rural people, so considering this move was a challenge to him. After considerable wrestling with God, we accepted the challenge, and we began this new phase of pastoral ministry.

Serving in Bindura for seven and a half years was one of the greatest periods of stretching and growing that we had ever experienced, with new challenges presented on a regular basis. The world at large perceived the problems in Rhodesia to be "merely" racial tensions or black vs white problems. Our work was with the two groups: white, English-speaking people and black Shona-speaking people. Could two races, involved in a bitter, dragged-out war, begin to understand each other, or even more remotely, love one another? How exciting it was for us to see, from first-hand experience, that Jesus is truly the Bridge Builder.

Wartime seems to get people actively thinking about God. They wonder if there really is such a being. If there is a God, how could He allow such a thing as war? Can a person really have a personal relationship with God? When one of our mining friends, who was not a believer, was dressed in combat uniform and ready to leave on a four-week stint of duty, I asked him if he ever thought about God.

His response: "Yes, when I am in a foxhole under fire and I am wondering if I will ever see my family again, I think of Him." With fighting and death so close at hand, people no longer had the luxury of sitting on the fence in their relationship with God.

Young men from both our English- and Shona-speaking congregations were called to defend their country, and many times it was against one another. Rhodesia was the bread basket of southern Africa. It is rich in minerals: silver, nickel, gold, copper, diamonds, platinum. Forces from Russia and North Korea and China were vying for control of the country. Each of those countries went to great expense to send weapons and finances, as well as abducting whole villages of young people who were taken to other countries to train and fight for their cause.

Sorrow and grief do not have a language barrier. The pain of losing a son in combat, or a daughter in a plane shot down by guerrilla bullets, or a child who dies when an ox cart hits a landmine is not different because of skin color or the language spoken. The heartache evident in the faces of the people during funerals was the same whether they sat in the pews of the old church during the English-speaking services or on the roughly hews logs in a renovated horse stable at a Shona service on a farm.

***

Our lives were challenged and blessed. We would never be the same as we saw the difference that Christ made in the lives of women and men who made Christ the Lord of their lives. One such man was Adrian.

Adrian was a handsome and tough Italian miner who took pleasure and pride in his times of combat, both in war-time experiences as well as in his personal life. When his wife, Pat, accepted Christ as her Savior, she began praying for Adrian's salvation as well. There were times in their marriage when many would say there were irreconcilable differences, but Pat chose to remain with him, hoping that her unbelieving husband would accept Christ, if she continued, by God's grace, to live a consistent life as a Christ follower.

After Pat had prayed and shared Jesus for seven years, Adrian visited us one night and said to Lynn, "I have decided that I cannot fight God any longer. Please tell me how I can become a Christ follower."

The list of victories in transforming lives of men and women could go on and on, each with their own unique story. As we recall each story, we are reminded of invaluable experiences with God as we learned to walk one step at a time, depending on Him for direction and guidance.

***

Highlighting our days during this time was the births of our four sons. Rick was born while we still lived in the tribal trust land, and Bradley came shortly after we moved to Bindura. Two years later we were very surprised to discover that God was going to give us another child. We sent letters to the grandparents in America to tell them that a caboose was to be added to the Everswick train. However, some weeks later, after a visit to the doctor in the capitol city, another letter had to be sent to them asking if they knew the plural of Caboose. The specialist confirmed that we were going to have twins. If I ever doubted the Sovereignty of God before, I certainly did no longer.

The news of the twins coming spread rapidly throughout our little town. Plans were made by the Greek community to expand our home, because they believed that twins were a special favor bestowed by God. The Greek families were the merchants of the town. They had not previously participated in our little church. One of the Greek families had had twins several years before and this "twinship" brought a special affinity with us. God used our twins as bridge builders. Even their birth was a community project because of the road ambushes, has curfews. Nevertheless, a crew of people was mobilized to give escort should it be needed for a nighttime trip to the hospital. Often there were false alarms: the team of six men would arrive at my house only to hear me say, "Sorry guys, the contractions stopped."

The war for independence continued to intensify. Ambushes, landmine explosions, and attacks on farms were occurring with alarming regularity. People from outside the country came into the local villages with threats if the villagers ever told anyone that they had come. They brought guns and ammunitions for insurrection. The atrocities committed on the local people were horrific. Acts of terrorism are just that...terrorizing. The frequency with which Lynn was called upon for funerals in both English and Shona communities was tragic.

Only a few weeks after he did the marriage of one young couple, we held a funeral for the husband who was killed in a road ambush. The son of a board member was killed shortly after the celebration of his 21st birthday. Another board member lost his daughter when her Viscount airplane was shot down. Lynn was once called to our nearby hospital to help a family being brought there by helicopter after being caught in an ambush crossfire. Each member of the family of four had been hit by bullets; some shattered the dad's leg and their four-year-old boy was killed. As Lynn carried him to the morgue and saw how much he looked like our precious Brad, who was the same age, his heart asked God for a fresh blessing for this dear family. Prayer without ceasing was a daily practice; we learned such deep dependence on Him.

Those were days when pat answers and old cliches just would not work. God had promised that we could call on Him in the days of trouble and that He would give strength, and He did just that. God did not fail us when our own words would not come. When our hearts felt like they were breaking with empathy, the presence of a living God filled the vacuum.

One night Lynn and I had to be at a school function. I was part of the PTA team serving dinner. Baba Friday was a wonderful African man who lived on our property, and he promised that he would check on the children for the few hours that we were going to be gone. Our daughter Kim was eleven, Rick, eight, Brad, three and the twins, Timothy and Brendon were just a year old. As parents, we had chosen not to emphasize all the horrors of the war, and we downplayed as much as we could. However, the children heard more than their share of the stories in school and all around them.

As we left that night, Lynn said to our daughter, Kim, "Baba Friday is right here. If you should hear any loud noises, please wake all the boys, put them in the hallways, and close the doors. Then lie still and quiet and we will get home as soon as we can." We were only a few blocks away. There had not been any wide-spread attacks on the town, but rumor predicted them, and he wanted to prepare Baba Friday and the children without alarming them.

Shortly after ten that evening, I had finished serving up the dinner at the school, and Lynn and I joined another couple to eat. Just then the loud noises began. I hadn't realized how loud mortars and machine guns could be until we were ourselves under attack. The town was surrounded with gunners in the hills all around us. No one could leave the school building, and we were advised to get to the floor and under the tables. As friends and I crawled under the small school tables, we started to pray for peace in the hearts of our children.

The promise of Paul to the Philippians became very real: *"Do not worry about anything, pray about everything, tell God your needs, and don't forget to thank Him for the answers; when you do this you will experience a peace from God that the world knows nothing about"* (Philippians 4:6,7 LB).

Could God provide that peace for our young daughter who was at home with her four little brothers? The explosions were so loud; would the children be frightened? We personally felt the peace of God envelope us as we continued to pray under the table. But our prayer was for the kids, for peace as well as their safety as we waited.

With both incoming fire and outgoing retaliation, it was nearly twenty minutes before Lynn could be escorted to our home on an army vehicle. As he entered the house and went into the hallway, a precious huddle of pajama-clad little angels lay sound asleep on their pillows. As Lynn described to me later, it was the perfect picture of God's peace. Kim woke up, saw her dad and said, "Daddy, can we go back to bed now?" There was no fear and no tears for any of them. In the midst of the booms and bangs of machine guns, those precious boys obeyed their sister when they got out of bed with their pillows and promptly nestled down on the hard wooden floor and fell quickly back to sleep. They were enfolded in the arms of God and were experiencing "the peace of God, that the world knows nothing about" and we, their parents, once again had had a memorable experience with a God who loves us and cares for us every day.

The end of the war brought great relief. However, the coming to power of the Marxist government presented different challenges for both the black and white citizens of the new Zimbabwe. Could trust between the races be restored? What would happen to the economy? There had been such intense fighting for so many years that it was difficult to comprehend a complete reversal almost overnight. Guns and ammunition were no longer an accepted way to solve the differences between the groups of people. The language barrier still existed and the cultural barrier was more noticeable than before. The government was being run by people with Marxist influence who each wanted control of the country and all its resources. Their goals and methods were different, but not necessarily wrong. Nothing seemed familiar.

13

Mariet's Prayer
Bindura

In 2019, on the 50th anniversary of our first trip to Zimbabwe, I posted a photo of Ellsworth on my Facebook page, again thanking those students for that amazing gift and token of faith on their part, a gift that blessed us incredibly.

The post about Ellsworth and the faith of those students brought comments from people all over the world. Each comment was significant, but there was one in particular that impacted us.

Susanna, from South Africa wrote: "Lynn and Judy, because of those young people sending you to Africa, our family's path crossed with yours in the town of Bindura, and we were changed forever."

Susanna's mom, Mariet, was an amazing woman of faith. She loved God with all her heart. Her family belonged to a Dutch Reformed church that met in our town every other week. On the alternate weeks Mariet and her children attended our Fellowship. Mariet was a fabulous cook and a consummate hostess.

The little church that Lynn began pastoring was missing their usual times of fellowship with others because of the challenges of being on the roads. Being isolated and almost sequestered in their homes or on their farms during these days of political tension was hard on everyone. Lynn and I talked about solutions, and we decided to have what we called Family Days.

Every few weeks, right after church, we would head out to a different farm to the family who had offered to host. Grills were set up and everyone brought their own meat to cook on the fires. Families brought food of all varieties to share. The generosity of the people soon had the tables laden with delicious food. A favorite drink for everyone was something that we called Fellowship Punch. I used a huge green plastic basin and I would fill it with a base that I made out of boiled Zimbabwe tea and then would dissolve sugar while the tea was still hot. There was no set recipe and the punch changed by the season each time it was made. Most of the surrounding farms were commercial enterprises; their produce and fruit were sent to market, but there was always an abundance for sharing. Whatever fruit was in season, everyone would set aside any excess and puree it, put it in plastic bags, and freeze it. When it was time for a Family Day, anyone who had the frozen fruit puree would bring their plastic bags, and we would cut them open and put the frozen chunks in the big green basin. When everyone had put in their contribution, we would add a few bottles of ginger ale. The taste of the punch changed from season to season, coinciding with whatever fruit happened to be available. It was a community project, and everyone felt a part of making the delicious and healthy concoction. Hence it was called Fellowship Punch.

***

The Family Days became one of the highlights of our town life. Because of the political situation and the economic boycotts, there were shortages of fuel, food and other necessities. Everyone was feeling stressed. The sweet time of fellowship on Sunday afternoons served to change the times of stress to times of food, fun, and laughter. An attitude of gratitude replaced the fear and despondency of the political climate. The laughter around the volleyball courts or the friendly enthusiasm of lawn-darts competition was something that bonded us deeply.

However, with the 4 PM curfew on the roads, the time to gather always seemed too short. One Family Day, I decided to combine a baby shower for one of the young women having her first baby. The ladies all gathered inside to celebrate the upcoming birth of Sharon's baby. I asked Mariet if she would close our time in prayer and bless that birth. Before she ended her prayer, she leaned over and pulled her 8-year-old son, Charlesy, close to her. He was the youngest in their large family and was a smiling, happy boy who brought joy to anyone near him. Mariet asked God to use the life of her little boy to be a blessing to all those he met, but especially in the life of her husband. After that time of prayer, we went outside, hugged, and piled into our cars and trucks to head back to our respective homes. We traveled in convoy from the farm, and the cars and trucks would peel off as they reached their own farm roads. We probably lived the furthest from the farm.

As we drove into our driveway, we could hear the phone ringing in the house. I rushed to answer it. It was a call from the local hospital a few blocks from our home. "Please send Pastor Lynn to the hospital ASAP."

When Lynn arrived, he heard the horrific news. When Mariet and the family arrived at their farm, Charlesy had been carrying the family UZI. It was a small automatic weapon, made in Israel, that could literally fit under his little arm. It was small, but it was as lethal as a larger weapon. Charlesy was running into the house, tripped on the root of a large tree, and the gun had an accidental discharge. He had been shot in the head–an incredibly horrible accident! Lynn sat in the hospital with Mariet, who was holding the head of her dear little boy and watching as the monitor indicated his life was ebbing away. They prayed together for Charlesy. Through tears of pain, Lynn shared scriptures from the Bible of God's promises like Psalm 23: When we walk through the Valley of Death, He promised to be with us.

Philippians 4:6 reminds us to pray about everything and tell God our needs, but the next verse reminds us to thank Him for the answers. Sometimes those answers are not exactly what we were expecting or praying for. As Charlesy's life faded away, and he was transported into the arms of the God that he loved so much, Mariet whispered to Lynn, "It has hardly been an hour since I prayed that God would use the life of my little boy to bring Glory to God. This was not at all what I was expecting, but I trust God so much, and I know that God doesn't make mistakes."

Her heart was breaking, but she was remembering the scripture and promises found in the verses Lynn had shared.

> *Don't worry about anything.*
> *Pray about everything.*
> *Tell God your needs.*
> *Remember to thank him for answers.*
> *And when you do this,*
> *you will experience the peace of God*
> *that the world knows nothing about.*
> *Philippians 4:5-7.*

Lynn did that very difficult funeral a few days later. He too felt God's presence as he shared with many students from the school as well as with Charles, the dad. A few days later, Charles made a commitment to become a follower of Christ. Without a doubt, that young boy's life brought glory to God.

***

Through the faith of a great bunch of high school kids in Staten Island NY, raising money to buy us airplane tickets to Africa, combined with the complete faith of a grieving mom who was completely confident in the Sovereignty and Goodness of the God she trusted, Lynn's and my faith grew as well. Stories of remembrance of God's faithfulness are important. Write your stories down; remind yourself and your children of those times when God has shown His faithfulness; your faith will be renewed in so doing.

14

Alison And Ambush Alley

One of the blessings of our move to Bindura, Zimbabwe, in 1976, was that farmers had begun to turn their lives to Christ. When we had to leave Kapfundi because of the dangers of the ensuing war of liberation, our concern was that our ministry would be only to white, English-speaking people. What we found was that as the farmers came to Christ, they had a desire that their staff and farm laborers would also come to know Jesus.

Shortly after we moved in to our new home, Lynn began weekly meetings on one of the farms in the Mtepetepa region. It was about a 25-mile drive through the rolling hills that surrounded our town.

Reggie Chitsuru was the organizer and local contact for the group that was meeting on the Homan farm. Reggie was an amazing African believer. He was the father of nine children who all lived in the farm compound with him. Despite Reggie's crippling arthritis, there was always a bright smile on his face. He was the foreman of the Homan Chicken Farm and an exceptionally hard worker. Sharing God's love was of utmost importance to him. After work and on weekends, he would ride his bike for miles to areas all around to have Bible studies with families on other farm compounds. Unbeknownst to him, his testimony was reaching further than only to the Africans who shared his language.

One day there was a knock on our front door. Standing before me was a beautiful young woman, almost hidden behind a stack of 10 dozen egg trays. She introduced herself to me. "Hi, you don't know me. My name is Alison, and I live in the Mtepete-pa district. Your husband comes out to meet with Reggie, our chicken farm foreman. I am the farm owner, but despite his being poor and struggling with arthritis, Reggie has something in his life that I do not have. Can you tell me what it is?"

Alison went on to share with me that she was an atheist; she did not believe in God nor the Bible. She had been a philosophy major in college, and God did not fit into her equation. But, Reggie! She had seen a joy in him that despite his circumstances in life, she could not fathom or explain. "Please could you share with me, what you share with him."

That began a wonderful, exciting friendship and a surprising adventure watching God at work in Alison's life. She came to our home every Friday with eggs as a gift, and we would sit exploring the Word of God; digging for the answers to the questions that plagued her and her husband as well. After about six months of our weekly visits, Alison said one day, "I would like to become a child of God and be assured of my salvation."

What a day that was! Through tears of joy, we prayed together and she joined God's family. I personally learned much during those days of digging in God's Word, but more importantly, Allison committed her life to the One who loved her so much.

Almost immediately, Allison's concern turned towards her husband and her friends in the farms around her. How could they learn about Jesus? They didn't have that same initial interest that Allison had that would cause them to drive to town to my house. Most didn't attend church. She asked if I would consider going out to the district each week to meet with a group of ten women. Alison asked that we call it a discussion group on life; she thought that the farm wives would not come to a Bible study. The farms in Mtepetepa were huge commercial outfits and were spread out through a large area. They were quite isolated from one another, so the ladies always looked for a reason to get together.

The farming community at Mtepetepa was, for the most part, very affluent. The farmers were successful and had all the material things that one could wish for. Zimbabwe was known as the bread basket of southern Africa. The farmers worked hard, but also played hard. The country club was the center of activity, and drinking and partying were their outlets on the weekends.

The battle for independence in the country came vehemently and violently. There were other countries, like Russia and North Korea, who were pouring resources and weapons into the country to gain access to the minerals that could be found. Almost everything that could be mined is found in Zimbabwe: Gold, platinum, copper, diamonds, nickel and the country's soil was very rich for crops. Countries were vying to take over Zimbabwe. When the fight for governance came, it hit the farming community hard.

The road out to Mtepetepa was affectionately known as Ambush Alley. It was hilly and the roads were winding but the view was breathtakingly gorgeous. That road was also an easy target. Ambushes were frequent. It was easy for gunners to stand strung along the road about 10-15 feet apart and strife a moving car or truck with bullets then run into the hills. On one occasion we were called following an ambush on the Mtepetepa Road. A mom and dad and their two little boys were hit in the ambush. Their car made it out of the attack and came to a halt a little way down the road. A nearby farmer heard the noise, called the army, and a helicopter soon reached them. Lynn was called to meet them at the hospital. The mom and dad and one of the sons were wounded. The youngest child, a little blonde boy the same age as our son, had taken a bullet through his heart. Lynn's own heart felt that it had been ripped from his chest as he had to carry this precious boy to the morgue. "Why God? How do I respond, God?" Tears and hugs were a soothing balm, but they were not the only answers.

Our hearts ached for the atrocities performed on the inhabitants of the villages. Our mission doctor was brilliant. Although just a trained GP and surgeon, not a plastic surgeon, he became skilled at repairing lips or ears that had been cut off. The villagers were threatened never to speak a word of the terrorists' visits. Many of these "freedom fighters" were just young teens. Whole villages were abducted and taken to other countries. Many were just given daga–drugs to make them numb to what was being done to them. They did unimaginable things to the people to keep them quiet and keep them from sharing their locations to the local police and army. I can't even bring myself to write of the other atrocities. How do people stoop to this level?

Alison asked me to meet with the farm wives, so I drove each week on the Mtepetepa Road. Growing up in Long Island and taking buses and subways from the age of fifteen to work in Lower East Side of New York prepared me for that drive to Mtepetepa. The drive, gorgeous and picturesque, took about 45 minutes. Each Tuesday, I would take our 18-month-old son, Bradley, with me while the two older children were at school. I wanted to be finished with Bible study no later than 3:30, so that we could get back on the road and have most of the trip done before the 4 PM curfew.

The discussion group with the ladies was fascinating. Some already had a relationship with God, and for others, the conversation was something brand new. We met for many months as a discussion group, and then began studying the Bible as some women were rededicating their lives to Christ and some were just choosing to follow Him. It was encouraging and thrilling to see the hunger and thirst for God's word. It is easy to sit on the fence in one's relationship with Almighty God when one is living the good life and there are no devastating circumstances around. But, when there is uncertainty and danger pressing in around you and friends are being ambushed and killed, one's mortality becomes the new reality. People started thinking more about God and about life after death.

Driving through Ambush Alley was actually one of the highlights of my week, and the time I spent with those ladies, a precious highlight of my life as a missionary.

About ten months into my drives, I found out that I was pregnant with twins. Needless to say, that was a huge shock to me! I had had severe morning sickness with our first three children, and this pregnancy proved to be no different, except that it continued for five months rather than the usual three. My pregnancy coincided with the Zimbabwe rainy season. That proved to be a bit of a challenge. The road to Mtepetepa was often flooded over during the rainy season. The alternative to the washed-out road was crossing the river on foot on a wooden, slatted swing bridge.

Judy and Bradley on the swinging bridge

I hadn't told any of the women at the Bible study that I was pregnant. We made a plan because my little Peugeot 504 could not traverse a raging river. One of the ladies very kindly offered to meet me at the other side of the river when it was in flood. I would leave my car on one side and carry Bradley in one arm and my basket of Bible study books and materials on my other arm. I can still feel my queasiness and wretchedness as I walked across that spindly bridge. It seemed a mile long. The bridge was not super sturdy, with wooden slats spaced a several inches apart. The handrails were just rope to hold on to for stability, but both my arms were full. As the river raged tumultuously beneath me, and my "all day morning sickness" was still active, it seemed like a very long walk to reach the other side. The friend who was meeting me surely wondered about my green complexion. I could not keep the news of my pregnancy quiet much longer.

God's fingerprints were all over that newly-formed Bible study with those ten brave farmers' wives. Their hunger for truth and security in Christ made the trip out to them worthwhile.

My twin babies grew quickly inside me. Once the ladies knew about the babies, they insisted on making the drive in to my house rather than my driving. By then I could hardly fit behind the steering wheel of my car. What a sacrifice on their part! They were counting the cost of making the decision to follow Christ and learning more about Him by coming to a Bible study. Most of the ladies by this time were driving vehicles with lead plating along the bottoms to protect from land mine explosions. Their trucks and cars were outfitted with bullet-proof glass. Those heavy vehicles got only 5-6 miles to a gallon of gas. During this time of sanctions, fuel was $6 or $7 a gallon, so the cost to them was high. The next "cost" was the arguments that arose from many husbands who were not believers and not very excited about their wife's new-found faith. They did not encourage the women to make the dangerous drive.

Allison and the Yellow Submarine

The ladies truly counted the cost of traveling Ambush Alley. Instead of one car going out their way, 7-8 vehicles were coming in to town. A few of the farms were close enough for women to car pool. Most of the ladies would arrive at our house with six shooters on their hips and FN rifles in tow. All the vehicles would park on my front lawn; it made quite a dramatic display. The ladies, dressed up in their pretty sundresses, would pile their weapons in the corner of our living room. Tea and snacks and fellowship had always been a vital part of our time together. The ladies would take turns making yummy treats each week and the much-needed time chatting with one another was very special. But it was decided later that we would forego the tea and snacks and get straight into studying the Word so to have enough time for discussion and questions and still get to the safety of their farmhouses before dark.

Weapons and walkie-talkies always close

Jill, who had to drive directly past the entrance to Alison's farm, picked Alison up. Alison would wait at the end of her long, winding road in her vehicle and hop out when her friend came by. On the way back, she was dropped off at the end of her road, and her farm driver was there to pick her up in what we affectionately called her Yellow Submarine. It was a bright yellow, armored, landmine-proof Land Rover. She waved goodbye to Jill, and got into her own vehicle. One day, she and the driver got about a mile down the road when the Yellow Submarine started sputtering--apparently out of gas. There were no cell phones, so the driver walked the mile or so back to the farm house to get fuel. Alison knew that there had been a gang of terrorists in the area the night before, and she did not feel comfortable walking on that road. She decided that she would stay in the field and wait for the driver to return. Knowing that there were armed men in the area could have/should have been a bit nerve wracking. Alison had been studying God's Word. From the very beginning of her commitment to God, she had taken every single word of the Lord literally, especially about the importance of putting trust in God's hand. She knew He said she must trust Him in all things, and so she did.

Alison found a low rock in the middle of the field and decided that she would sit down and talk to the God about her situation. She told me that before coming to faith in Christ, she would have been filled with fear. But God had promised her peace, so she would just wait on that rock and pray until the driver returned. After spending quite a while in prayer, she heard the vehicle returning. The surprise that she was not expecting was the way God chose to protect her. Cows are known to be very curious animals. While she was sitting on that rock praying, all the cows in the field came over and surrounded her. She was confident that if the freedom fighters walked by, she could not have been seen surrounded by God's beautifully created, curious cows.

It was several years later that Alison's husband Richard came to Christ. He was in Australia when his heart was opened to hearing the Word. Alison's years of prayer for him were rewarded. Praise God!

Over and over during our days of serving, God never ceased to surprise us with His fingerprints on our lives as well as on the lives of the people that we met on our own life's journey. Reggie, Alison, Richard, and the farm wives were only a few. Although we passed through some dangerous places, we did not live in fear, for we know the One who has us and to Whom we belong.

15

We Had The Twins!

The due date for the twins was October 1. The plan was to have the addition done before they arrived, but things always go a bit slower than expected in building, but the foundation was beginning to be poured when I went to the capital city, about an hour away, for a doctors appointment. It was still more than a month before they were due to deliver when I once again went into labor again. I was rather huge and was so happy that they were coming, even if a month early. Lynn was with me when we checked in but the doctor decided it was too early, so he successfully put me out of labor, but would not let me out of the hospital. The dangerous roads, and the size of the babies, he felt it was best to keep me right there.

Lynn returned to our home in Bindura with the three children and I stayed put, for ten more days. Lynn had a lot on his plate with the three kids and construction on the house and he was trying to sell our car, a gorgeous Peugot 504. It was without a doubt the nicest car we had owned, but it would definitely not hold seven of us. We were still in days of big rationing and finding a larger vehicle was a challenge.

Ten days in hospital was for sure an eternity, but one evening I knew that the labor pains were for real, but since I was already in the hospital, I decided I would keep it a bit of a secret til the last minute so that no one could change their mind! Lynn was doing a camp back in Bindura, and had no access to a phone, so no way to let him know what was up. Meanwhile back at the hospital I was walking, doing jumping jacks and anything else I could think of to get those babies delivered. I finally walked over to the labor ward about an hour after labor started, and could tell the babies were ready to come. We didn't know their sex, but we were blessed with two boys, born 12 minutes apart, seven and eight pounds. Lynn found out the next morning and he and the kids drove in to meet them.

In Zimbabwe hospitals, the mom and baby are kept in for seven to ten days, and that was good to have a few days to get used to the new paradigm, but it was finally time to go home and I was excited about that. Lynn was able to easily sell our Peugot, but then was unable to find any cars on the market. To my surprise, he picked the three of us up in a cute little VW bug. We definitely would not have passed any baby restriction rules as we left the hospital. We put the twins top to toe in a little carry cot bed, behind the back seat of the little VW, and the other three in the back seat. We were like that for several months until Lynn was able to get a VW combe with a little more room. The day after we returned from the hospital, the construction workers broke through the bedroom wall for the added bedroom and bathroom for the house, and when it was completed it was such a blessing. Such an unexpected gift from the community. We had such thankful hearts.

An Attitude of Gratitude; a lesson we continued to learn every day. The blessings and challenges of life are so affected by how we ourselves perceive things and when we look through the lens of thankfulness.

16

Furlough 1980

More than ever before, Lynn and I were excited about our ministry of being bridge builders. Our five-year term had almost come to an end, and we were expected to return to the USA for a required year-long furlough. We had some misgivings about leaving at that time. We received permission from our mission to delay our furlough for two years to stay in Zimbabwe for a seven-year term, but they advised us to confirm that decision with the schools our children were attending.

Each year of high school built upon the prior years. At the end of their four years, the students took cumulative exams of the four years' work. The Headmaster of Kim's school suggested that we stick to our original plan and go back to the states so that Kim's four-year high school career would not be interrupted, and she would not miss one of those important building blocks. So, it was decided that we would return for furlough at our regularly-scheduled time.

Our organization requires missionaries, when they first arrive back in the USA, to have a physical examination. The doctor pronounced Lynn in excellent health. The only thing that he noticed was a large black spot on Lynn's neck, so he suggested that it should be removed as soon as possible.

We scheduled a biopsy, and I must admit we did not think much of it. It was cared for and we thought no more about it. A week later, I brought the three younger boys in for their physicals. The doctor asked to speak to me alone. He informed me that Lynn's black spot was in fact a melanoma. It was already in the second stage. The doctor said that because the melanoma was located on his lymph glands, Lynn had a 25% survival rate. He requested that I bring Lynn in a few days later to discuss the options.

Shaken, frightened and bewildered, I drove home with the boys. The thought of losing Lynn, my husband and the father of five, was daunting. I drove home thinking of ways to break the news to him. After lunch, when the little ones were down for naps, I told Lynn the doctor's prognosis.

The first words out of his mouth were, "Judy, God has never made a mistake in our lives. We have just been through a very tense war for the past years. God was with us every step of the way. With all of the ambushes, and landmines and attacks, God could have taken either of us at any time. God has been with us and I am sure that He is with us now. Healing is within God's power if that is what He wants. But if he should choose to take my life, He will care for you and the children just as He always has."

Together we went back to those same verses in Philippians that we loved, and shared our needs with God. We once again experienced the peace of God that the world knows so little about.

The second surgery was successful in removing all the cancer cells; the margins were clear. The surgeon told me that the neck near the glands is typically a dangerous area for that kind of cancer, so it was good that he had surgery when he did. I asked the doctor how much longer it would have been until the cancer had spread to the lymph nodes and the rest of his body. He replied that there was no way of knowing, but that six more months would probably have been too late. God doesn't make mistakes. If we had had our way and remained in Zimbabwe that extra time, who knows what the outcome would have been.

***

Perhaps each of us has experienced times in our lives when we felt stubborn and determined to do things our own way. Lynn had accepted three challenges from our field council that he never wanted to do: manage local schools, be house parents in the boarding school caring for missionary kids, and work with the white people in Bindura. However, taking on those three challenges produced incredible growth in both Lynn and me. We went back to Zimbabwe in 1981, healed physically and bolstered spiritually.

Our family on furlough

17

Transitions

It was interesting that whichever way we were traveling: America to Africa, or Africa to America, it was always a bitter sweet time. It was hard to leave people that we loved, but we were also eager to see people on the other side. When I was sharing that with our International Director, Dick Winchell on day he said, "Judy you would have it no other way. It means that you have invested in and love the people you are with." Dick was right.

This time was no different. We left the USA with sad good-byes, but soon we were back into our home in Bindura and into our routine again.

Our first order of business was buying school uniforms for all the kids. All five had grown in the year so we had to get everything new. Our town of Bindura did not have a high school. Every student who finished 7th grade in Bindura and wanted to further their education had to take entrance exams and apply to high schools of their choice. Lynn's brother, Dale, lived in a town that had an excellent boarding school, and Kim decided that was where she would like to attend. It was a three-hour drive through a winding mountain pass and with 6 AM to 4 PM curfews still in place, it was a bit of a challenge trying to time the trips. The first time we left Kim was unbelievably hard for us, and I can remember mailing the first letter to her before we even left her town. Kim did very well at the school in both academics and sports, and the school felt like a good fit.

The missionaries would gather annually for a business conference in May. At the 1982 conference, Lynn was asked to stand for election as field leader. Uncharacteristically for Lynn, he declined taking the position. He felt that our work in the town of Bindura was thriving, and we were happy to be back in that setting. We had just settled Kim in a new high school. The timing was just not right.

However, the following months after he had declined the position, his heart was not at ease. He felt that he had asserted his own will, and perhaps had not followed God's leading. Lynn was not himself for sure and there was an unusual restlessness in him for many months.

In mid-December of that year, Lynn came to me and said, "Judy, I feel like perhaps that I have made a mistake. Men and women that I respect chose me to do a job, and I refused to do what I personally thought was best. If ever again men of God feel that I am well suited for a position, I believe I will more carefully consider it." My Lynn was back! The restlessness was gone. That issue had been settled for him and he was at peace.

However, just a few weeks later, after Christmas, his resolve was put to the test. The international Director of our organization flew from Wheaton, Illinois to Zimbabwe and specifically asked if he and his wife could spend some time in our home. What an honor that was; we were delighted. We loved them and looked forward to having time with them.

When the Winchells came, we told him that Lynn needed to go to put our car on the petrol line. During those many years of conflict, there were huge shortages of almost everything. Groceries, petrol and clothes were hard to get. Scores of people would go early in the evening and place their car in line at the petrol station. The cars were left so that the next morning, when the fuel trucks would come in, it was first-come-first-serve. If you were not served when the fuel ran out, you would walk back to the petrol station and take your car home to leave again a day or two later when the next fuel truck was expected. However, this particular night, Lynn was gone with Mr. Winchell until very late, and I was wondering where they were.

When the two men returned, they said to me, "We need to talk." The Board of Directors back in the USA had made a decision the previous May (at almost the same week that Lynn was declining to serve as Field Chairman) that they would like Lynn to return to the Chicago area and become an International Director over the countries of Pakistan, India, Sri Lanka, and the United Arab Emirates. This would normally not be an easy decision for Lynn. Zimbabwe was his home. His parents moved there when he was only 18 months old. But, just a couple of weeks prior, he had settled the internal battle in his heart. Now there were men and women that he respected asking him to leave Africa and settle in America. Lynn and I talked and prayed for some time and difficult as it was, we made the decision to accept this new opportunity.

For me, it was probably one of the hardest things I had ever done to be obedient to God. I was 16 when I committed my life to serving God in Africa. I had absolutely no desire to return to the USA.

We were asked not to tell anyone about this decision until May, five months later, when our organization had their Annual Conference, so that it could be shared with everyone at the same time. The plan was to have us leave Zimbabwe in August. It was heart wrenching for all of us. We began giving away most of our belongings and packed only three big boxes to take back to the states. Those boxes held our most precious things: photos, letters, trophies, farewell gifts, etc. but everything else was left in Africa.

The three boxes contained the totality of our earthly possessions. We packed them up in early August, giving us time to spend the last few weeks with the people we loved so much. Each farewell, whether in a little African church or the Bindura fellowship was difficult because we had invested so much of our lives there. War bonded us and each group was like family. We were confident that we were following the path that God had set before us, but it made it no less difficult to say those good-byes.

***

We arrived in Chicago to start a new life. In Zimbabwe, schools started in January, whereas in the US, they started in September. The children started in three different schools just a week after we landed. In Zimbabwe they wore uniforms to school; in the US, we had to buy new clothes and shoes. We had a total of $5,000 to our name to buy a house, a car, furniture, dishes, pots and pans, sheets, clothes, and shoes. We literally were starting from scratch. The fun and amazing part is that God provided for every single need from the most unexpected places.

Every week I waited for the shipping company to call and say, "Your boxes have arrived and they are ready for you to pick up." That call did not come. Month after month, I waited expectantly. It seemed like all of our treasures were gone for good.

Lynn's first weekend at his new job that August was a retreat, so he was gone three days; the following week he left for a conference in Colorado; and four days later, he left for four weeks in India. For much our first six weeks back in America, Lynn was gone. I was trying to get the kids settled in totally unknown territory.

Schools were so different. We didn't have a church home, and I personally felt like God had put me on a shelf. I had been super active in Zimbabwe with three ladies' Bible studies, PTA, so many wonderful friends, being the pastor's wife, and being a partner in ministry with my husband. Now, I was trying to hold it together for me and the kids, mostly by myself. All five of the kids were troopers, and I know it was not easy for them, but I was (and still am) so proud of them.

To be honest, I was mad at God for bringing us back to the States. My attitude stunk. Mrs. Winchell had urged me, "For the sake of your children, even if it means faking it, don't let them realize how much you don't want to be in here. You will recover at some point, but you don't want them to absorb your negativity." I did a lot of faking; I was *oh, so happy to be here* and *not* feeling the challenge of Lynn's long frequent overseas trips.

February 13, 1984–a long six months of being mad at God. God was trying to lean in to me. I was not cooperating. That February evening, we went to a meeting at which Lynn was speaking to a group of 50 or more college and university students. I remember his message almost verbatim. He shared with those students the story of Hannah in the Bible. That dear woman was desperate to have a child. She waited and waited for years and still she was faced with infertility. Then she started to beg God, and she finally bartered with Him and made a promise. "God, if you give me a son and let me raise him until he is weaned, I will give him back to you; and he can serve you in the temple, but please let me at least have one son."

God answered Hannah's prayer. She had a baby boy.

And Hanna fulfilled her promise to God. When he was weaned, Hanna went to the temple and presented Baby Samuel to the priest and let him live at the temple serving God. Oh, I can't imagine giving up any of my children. Each year following, when she made her pilgrimage to the temple, she made a little coat for her boy, reminding her son of her promise to God and of a mother's love

Lynn looked intently into the eyes of those college students. "Have any of you ever made a promise to God and then reneged on that promise?"

For me the room stood still. The only sound I could hear was the beating of my own heart. *He was speaking to me!* I squinted open my eyes while Lynn was praying, and he wasn't looking in my direction, but it sure seemed like he was directing his question to me. In the silence that followed, as Lynn let the students mull over that question, I knew what my problem was. I had given God a promise as a 16-year-old that I would serve Him whenever, wherever, however He wanted me to. Did wherever mean only Africa, or did it refer to serving God in the USA as well? My promise to God was not limited to geography. I knew the answer and that night made a recommitment to serve God anywhere! It was like a ton of weight fell off my shoulders. I was done fighting God. I wanted to be 100% in sync with where he wanted me.

It seemed like miracle after miracle happened that same week. I had not been asked to be involved in anything for six months– in direct contrast to how involved I was in Africa. That following Tuesday, the church we were attending asked if I would teach a ladies' Bible study. A few days later, I was asked to speak at a retreat for women. But the hardest to believe was after six months of being told to file insurance claims for the missing boxes, I received a call from Schipol Airport in Amsterdam. They told us that they found the missing three boxes way in the back of the airport cargo area. They were covered with dust, but all three were there. Amid apologies, they told us that the boxes would be shipped to us that week.

Wide open doors set before us. It didn't take much to figure out why there had been no speaking opportunities or why we didn't have our missing boxes. They contained the all-important memories that I had been clinging to. I was mad at God. I had a rotten attitude. God was tenderly and patiently waiting for me to surrender my will and my attitude to Him. On February 13, I had a change in my heart and after an attitude and heart adjustment, He was ready to work through me again.

18

Family

When we left Africa in 1983, Lynn was asked to take the new position in Chicago. It was hard for our family. Lynn had spent all of his growing-up years in Rhodesia (now called Zimbabwe). After we were married, we served there together for almost 15 years. We went when Kim was two months old, and our four boys were born there. All of us had made amazing memories. Living during the war of independence for seven years in the town of Bindura, we made the friends who are as close as family.

During those days in Chicago, Lynn was traveling quite a bit in his position as an Area Director for Western Asia and Africa. He was planning a trip back to Zimbabwe and South Africa the summer of 1989. We had been back in the USA for six years and up until then, only Lynn had been able to return to Africa. My uncle passed away about the same time and left me a small inheritance. We talked it over as a family, and decided that since Lynn had to be working in Zimbabwe for three weeks that summer visiting missionaries, the children and I would try to buy some reasonably-priced airline tickets with that money and return to Africa for the summer and meet up when Lynn came there for work.

Lynn's parents and their four children were all missionaries. The families' times of serving in the field and all of our furloughs rarely overlapped. Having a family reunion of parents and siblings was virtually impossible. However, in the summer of 1989, Lynn's parents were retired but were sent back to fill a vacancy in the town of Bindura, where we had served.

With Lynn returning, and his parents going to Bindura, there would be a time that summer when the entire Everswick Family would be in Africa at the same time. If we could figure a way to get our kids and me to Africa, since Lynn was going to be there for work, we could actually have the whole family together for a week overlap. I managed to find some pretty inexpensive flights for our trip. It was the perfect use for Uncle Bill's inheritance gift.

Just before our overseas trip, we were moving into a new home, closer to the high school where I was working in Wheaton and where our kids attended school. The closing of the house was the day before the children and I were to leave for Africa. Some dear friends helped us make the move. We didn't have time to set up the whole house, but they insisted that I needed at least to return with the kitchen set up. The rest of the house was totally empty, with boxes placed in each room for us to unpack when we returned from our trip.

The children and I had an amazing time visiting with dear friends and family in our former home town of Bindura for almost a full month. We got to see old friends, ride horses, stay on farms, swim, and were taken on plane rides with our old friend Rob (which was what inspired our son Bren to be a pilot). We spent quality time with the people with whom we had developed relationships through the war years.

While there, I received a letter from the vice principal of the high school where I worked, asking if I would add the position of Director of Student Activities to my Career Counselor position. It was a lot to think about because it would be a full-time job, plus some. With Lynn traveling so much, I had wanted a part-time position so I could be home for our children. However,

Kim was now in college, and the boys were in middle and high school, so it seemed like a position that I could accept. I was to start just a few days after I returned from Africa.

***

The whole extended clan was going to drive to Lake Kariba for our reunion. Lynn was expected to join us on Sunday, and we would all leave on Monday morning. However, we went to the airport to meet him and were told his flight had been cancelled. Before internet it was hard to get information, so we had no idea where Lynn was. It was finally decided that we would all go ahead to the lake as planned, and Lynn would join us when he arrived.

It had been years since we had been together as a family, and it was such a special time, but it would have been nice to know when and if Lynn were going to be able to come for those short four days on this rare occasion.

Monday evening, we drove to a nearby hotel to call to find out if there was any word from Lynn. We were delighted to hear he was in the nearby country of Zambia and expected to arrive on Tuesday. Our brother-in-law, Chris, offered to drive me to meet Lynn in a town a few hours away–halfway for us all.

It was wonderful to see Lynn after being separated for a month. However, after a few minutes of hugging and chatting about his crazy routed and rerouted trip, Lynn told me that my dad had passed away on Sunday. I was devastated. The drive back to where we were staying was filled with tears. I was half a world away from my mom and my family, and I was aching.

We arrived at Lake Kariba; the whole family had stayed awake to see Lynn. We shared the news about my dad, Captain Sherman. Wednesday was somewhat of a somber day; we spent time reminiscing our memories of Grandpa.

I woke early the next morning and went back to the same hotel to call my mom. I told her that instead of staying for the month of August as planned, I was going to try to find flights to return the next morning to America to be with her and be there for the funeral. My mom said that since they had not been able to reach me, and they did not know how long we would be out of touch, they had decided to cremate my dad the day before. More tears on my part. I was such a Daddy's girl and could not believe I would never see him again, not even at his funeral. But at my mother's urging, I accepted that she was planning a special memorial for him after I returned. She urged me to stay and return as scheduled

We had one more day together making Everswick family memories, and then we all returned to the capital city of Harare on Thursday. On the weekend, we visited friends, and Lynn preached at our former church. Then the whole church came together for a big family day. Lynn and I were to leave very early Monday morning to fly to South Africa for his work of visiting and encouraging the missionaries. Our five kids were going to spending those two weeks with friends on the farms. Most of the people in the church had met my dad during his two visits here, so there was a shared grief. There was no place I would rather have been that week than with our Everswick Family and the special people of Bindura who were like family.

We wanted to get to bed early before our morning flight, but at 10 PM there was a phone call. Lynn's dad woke us up–the call was for me.

My oldest brother, Bill, was calling to tell me that my mother had had a massive stroke alone at her house the night before, on Saturday night. She was found the next morning by a friend who was picking her up for church. Bill said that my mom was in a coma and not expected to live. I told him that we were supposed to leave tomorrow at 6 AM for work in South Africa, but that I would change my flight to go directly home to the USA. He insisted that I carry on because he was sure that my mom would not live another day. He thought that by the time I got home, she would be gone, so he urged me not to change my flight.

I was distraught, not knowing what to do. This was without a doubt the hardest decision I had ever been faced with in my life. We left as scheduled the next morning for Johannesburg and planned for me to call as soon as I got there. I could fly home from Johannesburg.

I know that I was neither mentally nor emotionally present for either the news of my dad's passing a few days before or my mom's stroke and coma. I called my brother from each city we visited, and he kept reporting the same–she won't make it through today, so just stay there. It was very expensive in those days to change tickets, but I was aching to be there with Mom.

When I called the next day from Capetown, my brother, George ,answered the phone. "Yes, Mom is still in a coma and still alive," and then he asked sharply, but with compassion, "What are you thinking, Judy? Come home immediately. Mom is staying alive until she hears your voice and knows you are there."

More tears, but relief for the very clear decision that was made for me!

It wasn't easy to get last-minute tickets. I had to go through France and overnight in an airport hotel there. The circuitous route took 50 hours to get to JFK airport. Lynn's brother Doug picked me up and drove me straight to the hospital. Mom didn't open her eyes when I went to her bed, but when I took her hand and told her I was there, she let out a very loud, guttural sound. We all believed it meant, "I know you are here, Judy." My brother George had been sitting at her side for five days, and he said it was the first sound that she had made.

George and I sat with her for days. I finally convinced him to drive back home to Vermont to tend to his animals and some things there, not knowing how long Mom would be with us. He had been with Mom after Dad passed away. and drove back to Vermont a few days after Dad's cremation, at Mom's insistence. When she had the stroke the following day, he drove back to south Jersey to be with her.

After George left, I had a few days alone with Mom, reading Scripture and singing (poorly) to her. These were hard days, but the more Scripture I read to Mom, the more it ministered to me.

The Lord is my shepherd.
Though I walk through the valley of the shadow of death, YOU
are with me.
Through the many Psalms and passages of Scripture, I was
really not alone. I intensely felt the presence of my Abba, (the
Hebrew word for God, our heavenly Father) during those days
in the hospital. I felt like I had crawled up on my Father's lap as
He held me. With no one else to talk to, I felt God's comfort as I
had never experienced it before.

***

July and August are the cold months in Africa. Where Mom
was living, it was exceptionally hot. I had only winter clothes
in my bag, and here it was 90 degrees. When I was dressing
to go to the hospital one morning, I decided I could not wear
my wool turtle neck and toasty warm clothes. So, I borrowed
Mom's sleeveless blouse and cotton skirt. That day was the only
time she opened her eyes; she looked deep into my eyes, then at
my blouse and my skirt, then back up into my eyes. I think she
knew I was borrowing her clothes, which she would not have
minded one tiny bit. I laughed and tried to let her know why
I was dressed in her clothes. What a sweet moment! My mom
was such fun, and I knew that she enjoyed that interchange. She
never opened her eyes again, but I treasure that sweet moment.

Mom passed peacefully the next day, on a Friday morning. I
was there with her when she was welcomed home in heaven.

My siblings asked me to speak on behalf of the family at the
memorial service for our parents. (My siblings are not believers,
but, by this time, at 81, both my parents had come to faith.) We
were able to celebrate the lives of both of our parents at the same
time. Doing the service was hard, but it was also a blessing to
be able to remember them and share my appreciation for all they
poured into my life.

I went alone to our home in Illinois. Lynn and the kids would
be in Africa for another week. I had decided not to tell them

about Mom's passing, wanting them to enjoy their last week in Africa without the sad memory of having lost both grandparents so suddenly. We had finished organizing the kitchen before I left, but nothing else was done. I would be starting a new full-time job in a week, and I had a big house to turn into a home before my family returned. I grieved, and I got to work.

***

Just as God had provided for Elijah, He provided Sandy to be there for me. My friend picked me up at the airport, took me to their home and just let me "be." She brought food and water and cared for me. She listened when I needed to talk and was silent when I was processing. She allowed me the privilege to be still for days on end. How thankful I am for the comfort of that deep friendship and for Sandy who was so empathetic. God knew! Although I felt suddenly orphaned, God's provision was exactly what was needed at that time, and I am forever grateful. Thank you, ABBA, for seeing me where I was, loving and caring for me in so many ways.

19

Dayuma
Ecuador

When I was a little girl, my family did not attend church. A precious lady who lived across the street, Ann Pape, came over one day to ask my parents if they would let her take me to Sunday school at her church. My parents happily agreed to allow me and my two brothers to go with her. It was about a six-city-block walk, and each Sunday Mrs. Pape would wait for us outside our house, and we would walk to church with her and her children, Richard, Barbara, and Nancy. I attended church for years all through grammar and middle school.

In January, 1956, a rather shocking thing happened that rocked the Christian world. Five missionary men were speared and killed on a small Sand Bar in the jungles of Ecuador known as Palm Beach.

The Auca Indians, as they were called then, were known for their murders and hostility to outsiders. Books were written and were passed around at our church about the brutal deaths of these five men who attempted to befriend the Auca and take the Gospel to them. Books like *Through Gates of Splendor*, *The Journals of Jim Elliot*, *The Dayuma Story*, and *The Jungle Pilot* were a few that were written about that massacre.

During my years in high school, I think that I read every one of them. *The Dayuma Story* particularly impacted me. It increased in me an incredible desire to share Jesus's love with people who had never heard about Him. Dayuma was a sister of one of the men responsible for the deaths of the missionaries. Her face, a photo on the book cover, with her deep black eyes and long straight black hair was etched on my mind.

The Auca tribe were known to be killers. It was an expectation for every Auca that their life would most likely end by being speared, if not by the outsiders, by one from their own tribe. The Auca tribe was not very big, and their language was unique to their group of nomadic people and was not found anywhere else in the world. They were isolated from other tribes. They feared for their lives should they ever encounter an outsider. They lived off the land. The fruits and vegetables that grew around them were their main food or they killed monkeys and other animals with their poison darts.

The book told that Dayuma's father had recently been speared and killed by one of his tribesmen, as was very common. Dayuma was horrified by her father's death. It did not help that her mother told her that she could expect the same thing to happen to her.

Although her mom warned her that if she left the confines of her tribe, she would most likely be killed by foreigners, Dayuma convinced two girls to escape the tribe with her. She faced a danger in her village but decided that it could not be worse to be killed by those you did not know, any more than killed by your own people. Dayuma managed to escape with two friends, and moved to live with the Quecha tribe in another part of the Amazon jungles.

There were missionaries in the area where Dayuma settled. Before long, Dayuma made friends with Rachel Saint, a single missionary translator. A unique and special relationship was formed between the two young women. The more they got to know one another, the deeper their relationship grew. Dayuma became the first person in her tribe to experience and accept the love of God. As Dayuma talked to Rachel about her tribe, Rachel became more and more intrigued. She wanted to find a way to translate the language of the Waorani, the name the tribe was later given so they could disassociate from their Auca killer name. Before her death, Rachel was able to translate the New Testament, and many of the tribe became followers of Jesus.

As a teenager, I was fascinated by reading these stories. I had committed my life to God at the age of 15. Dayuma's story impacted me in a way that I would never have dreamed. A year after I committed my life to Christ, I heard a lady from Africa speaking about serving God there among people who had never heard of Him. I knew that was what was on my heart, and that burning desire started in my life after reading about Dayuma.

* * *

Many years later, in 1999, during our travels working for the church as Global Pastors, Lynn and I found ourselves in the country of Ecuador. We visited two families who were living there. One family, Rob and Barb, lived in the capital of Quito, and we spent a few amazing days there with them. We even got to watch a coup as it was taking place. We were walking one day to the capital and saw the police, with their shields and gas masks marching towards a group of protestors. We were nearby and it was pretty fascinating to watch. Lynn was catching it all on video as the police were walking towards us. A few minutes later, the crowds started running and attacking the police. The police turned and were trying to run away right towards where we were standing. Lynn was still videoing until Ron suggested it might be a good idea for us to run too. We kind of giggled later looking at the film Lynn had taken. Men marching; police protecting; crowd going wild and chasing the police; then us running and Lynn forgetting to turn off the camera. All we saw on the video was swishing grass as we ran as fast as we could.

The second family we were to visit was Sandy and Darrell. They lived in a much more remote place in the Amazon Jungle. Darrell was a pilot. When we were dropped off at a small air terminal in Quito, I was walking around the building and looking at the photos on the wall. All of a sudden, the penny dropped for me.

"Lynn, do you know where we are?"

"Yes, Judy, we are in Quito, Ecuador!"

"Yes, but this is the Nate Saint Air Center." Lynn had been in Zimbabwe during the 1950's, so I am sure he knew nothing about the massacre of the five missionaries.

My mind was flooded with memories of reading the books about the deaths of those five men on Palm Beach. In particular, I remembered that *The Dayuma Story* had inspired me to consider a life of ministering internationally. I reflected on seeing the photos of Dayuma. As I stood there reading the plaques on the wall, I got goosebumps thinking *I AM HERE* in that same country, in Nate Saint Air Center.

It was a thrill to meet and spend time with Sandy and Darrell at their mission station. We saw their ministry and enjoyed time with their family. One morning during our visit, Darrell asked if we would like to go on a medical flight with them. We were delighted to see their ministry first-hand.

We flew in a small Cessna and were amazed flying by the volcanos nearby, and flying over the jungle, and over the mighty Amazon. Even though we were in a different country, that same Amazon River was a mighty force in the country of Ecuador.

Darrell mentioned from the front of the plane that we were ready to land. The area was all jungle, and there was only a small air strip down below, and it seemed like it would be quite a feat to land there. Darrell buzzed the people down below to let them know that we were about to land and then completed a flawless landing on the tiny grass airstrip.

A large group of indigenous people came running up to the plane as it stopped. I can't explain the emotions that I felt when

I saw the first person who pressed her face to the little window of the plane. *It was the same piercing black eyes, the same long black hair of the woman who had impacted my life as a teen. It was Dayuma!* It had been 40 years since I had read her story. She was the first one from her tribe to commit her life to Christ, and now she was an evangelist among her own people. She was married and she and her husband were serving God faithfully at that same area of jungle where the missionaries were killed. God was using her to go into a place where her relatives had been known as killers. The tribe was now coming to Christ. The name of their tribe was changed from AUCA to WAORANI. Their lives had been changed through their relationship with Jesus.

Judy and Lynn with Dayuma

I was in awe of this privilege of getting to meet this precious woman. Dayuma asked if we would want to visit Palm Beach where the five missionaries were martyred. Could this trip be more amazing? We followed Dayuma to the river where we got into a dugout canoe. It was a hollowed-out tree trunk. Dayuma was at the bow to paddle, followed by Darrell, Sandy, Lynn and me, with Dayuma's husband paddling from the rear. Reaching Palm Beach was sobering. It seemed like hallowed ground, where men seeking to befriend the tribe who were known to be killers, had been killed. Back in the 1950's, when the story of their martyrdom came out, hundreds were challenged to give their lives to go to the "ends of the earth" to share Jesus's Love.

I was one of them.

What a momentous day for me. My call had come full circle. I was standing there on Palm Beach, reflecting on our years of serving God, and reliving the call that God had put on my heart so long ago. Thanks be to God.

20

Nazare and Doña Coraçao
Brazil

Our first visit to Brazil is imprinted on my brain as if it were yesterday. As Global Pastors, part of our job description was to visit our global workers wherever they served. In 1999, we took our first official trip for our church. The plan was to see six families serving in four different countries. One of the stops was with a wonderful couple, Kim and Rick and their two delightful boys. Their ministry was among the river people in the very remote area in Northern Brazil, in the city of Belem. Belem is where the great Amazon River flows east into the Atlantic Ocean. The majority of the people that live along the river have access to the outside world only by canoes or small outboard motor boats. As Kim and Rick explored the area, they found hundreds of families living along the tributaries of the Amazon. They built a small boat as their main mode of transportation. On the boat they had a small refrigerator, stove and hammocks where they could sleep on the boat as they traveled. They would venture out for days, and sometime weeks at a time to visit the families along the river.

During our visit, we had the privilege of accompanying Kim and Rick as they dropped off the Bible School students at various spots along the Amazon. The students stayed in the village from Friday to Saturday. Their time was spent getting to know people and building relationships. When it was agreed to by the village leaders, the students would teach the Bible and share God's Word with the villagers. It was such a privilege for us to meet the local people and enjoy their culture.

Soccer is huge in Brazil, even in the most remote village. It is a favorite pastime for both young and old. Interestingly, soccer is also one of Lynn's favorite sports. He enjoys getting to play as often as he can. Soccer is also the key that opened doors to connect with the people. I remember visiting in one very remote village on the river, and as we arrived, we saw a large group of people crowded around the open window of a very small basic hut. As we passed by, we saw that they were all watching a small tv that was hooked up inside the hut. The Brazil National team was playing, and there was much enthusiasm and cheering as they watched their favorite team.

The fauna and the variety of fruits of the Brazilian jungle were exquisite! Everywhere we walked there was some new kind of flower to admire or fruit to try. I remember Matt and Greg finding a fruit that I had never seen before. Inevitably, one of the boys would say, "Let Judy try it; she will eat anything." And I did love everything they handed me.

On Sunday, Lynn was asked to preach at a local church, with Rick interpreting. The two of them had a great rhythm as they preached and interpreted with a wonderful ease. After church, we enjoyed a big lunch of rice and beans and freshly caught little river shrimp. It was a great meal and we ate until we were quite full.

After lunch, Rick needed to go on the river to pick up the four Bible school students that we had left in the villages along the Amazon the previous Friday. Poor Kim was suffering from a migraine and felt that she needed to stay back; Lynn had been asked to play soccer with the dads and kids from the village after church and didn't want to pass up the opportunity to play. In the villages, soccer was played barefoot, so Lynn did the same. He was reminded of that decision a few days later as he found some interesting parasitical worms had made their way into the bottoms of his feet.

Before our visit, it had never occurred to Lynn or me that the Amazon had tides that coincided with the tides of the Atlantic Ocean, into which it flowed. In high tide, Rick could not take their bigger boat but to collected the students in his smaller motorboat.

When Rick asked if I would like to come along, I did not hesitate to accept. First, I was never one to miss an adventure, and second, my dad was a tugboat captain, and my happy place was on the water.

Sitting at the bow of the boat while we sped along the river was invigorating. Before we had gone too far though, the heavens opened and rain started pouring. I was drenched as the rain pelted down. The midday Brazilian sun, which had been scorching our skin when we first started out, was now hidden behind big dark clouds. I must admit though, it was cooling and refreshing having that heavy rain washing over our parched skin.

Our first pick-up was at a tiny little village, tucked along the banks of the Amazon. It belonged to a sweet and very generous woman named Nazare. The huge smile on her face when she saw Rick was a "tell-tell" of how much she appreciated his coming. The two male students were ready to leave, but Nazare had another plan. "Have you had lunch, Pastor Ricardo?" Rick knew that she must have prepared something special for him. "We would love to have lunch with you," he responded.

I said I loved adventure, and this was one I would not easily forget. Nazare invited us to sit down.

Her dining room table consisted of a plank of wood hammered on to tree stumps that were about waist height. The bench was another log, balancing on forked logs. It was simple and delightfully cozy. Nazare seemed to be so pleased to be offering lunch and didn't seem to mind that this foreign American lady was joining her. Nazare placed a high pile of rice on a metal plate. On top of the rice, she deftly plopped a very large, boiled river crab. The whole crab! It was so big that it hung over the sides of the plate. In spite of my dad's having been on the ocean and rivers and our growing up eating lots of seafood, I was unused to attacking a crab, especially one this big, with just my hands.

I always had used those nifty wooden crab mallets, or a shiny seafood cracker or metal pick. None of these were available at sweet Nazare's place. As I was looking at this huge crab, I was completely befuddled as to even how to begin. Ricardo was so busy eating his crab, that he did not seem to notice that I had not taken a bite. He was breaking off the legs, cracking them into pieces, deftly pulling out the crabmeat, and popping pieces into his mouth. Being a total novice at this seafood dining experience, I just sat there trying to find the best way to dig in.

However, Nazare DID notice. She said something to Rick in Portuguese and he responded. "No, this lady is an American. She has no idea how to eat tak tak." The name was the perfect onomatopoeia for the sound of the cracking and breaking as they ate this crab.

Quite amazed that I was such a novice, Nazare was the perfect hostess. She wiggled her little bottom between us as we were sitting on the tree trunk, and she took it upon herself to help me. As I mentioned before, the tiny villages dotted along the river only had access to the outside world by canoe or a small run-about boat with motor. Dentists were not available, I am sure, until much later when the Parkers blessed the people by bringing doctors and dentists to visit the river communities. Dear Nazare had probably never visited a dentist, and she was missing her four front top teeth and four bottom teeth. However, she was a woman of action. She picked up my crab, and quite easily broke off each crab leg, one by one in the back molars in her mouth and crunched down. A loud crack ensued as the shell of the crab split. She then pulled the cracked leg shell out of her mouth, removed the crab meat from the shell, and put it on my spoon or directly on the pile of rice. We proceeded to bond in a unique way, and I was able to eat the entire crab with her incredible help. What a delightful time we had!

The time was going fast and we needed to go on to the next village. The rain which had subsided while we were visiting Nazare started again. We had dried off but soon were drenched by the newest downpour.

Our next stop for students was to the village of Doña Coraçao. Kim had told me about this woman who was the head of her village. She was considered a witch doctor in the area, and she did not like Christians at all. When Kim and Rick were doing early research in the area, Doña Coraçao was not at all pleased that they were wanting to bring the Bible into her area. However, on one of their earliest visits, her granddaughter was very ill with a high fever. Rick took time and prayed over the girl, and soon after that time of prayer, her fever broke. Grandma's heart was softened and she was much more open to the Bible students coming to stay with her on the weekends. Her heart was still not open to God, but she had more respect for Rick's healing prayer.

Kim had shared quite a bit about her and I must admit that I was a little curious about meeting her. She sounded strong and antagonistic. As we were in the runabout, making our way to her village, I began imagining what she would be like.

There had been a significant change in the Amazon and the river communities since we had dropped off the students on Friday. Water was flooding over the banks and the tide had gone up. At high tide everything looked vastly different.

The rain was still pelting down when we arrived at our destination. It really did look different! On Friday, there had been a dock for us to off load the students. Now there was none. I am sure that I must have looked quizzically at Rick, even before I voiced the question, "How are we going to make the walk back to that village if there is no dock for us to climb on?" Where the dock had been, there were just big floating logs. There were also wet, soggy vines hanging from the trees. We were pretty drenched as well from this latest deluge.

Rick was non-plussed, as the situation was not new to him. "We will walk on the floating logs!"

REALLY, Rick? Wasn't that just at carnivals? Did he not know about all the movies I had seen with anacondas twisted around the vines in the Amazon jungle? Did he not know that piranhas, common in the river, probably love to chew on the arms and legs of crazy Americans (or anyone else) that happen to fall into the water? I was sure that he was pulling my leg about walking back to the village on rolling wet logs!

But no, he was not kidding and off we started. Rick asked the two Bible school young men to stay with the boat as it was sloshing about. Remember, I am not a fan of snakes that wrap themselves around you nor of the flesh-eating fish with the big sharp teeth; even the little snakes are not my personal favorites. But we stepped out. The logs were slippery. They kept moving and rolling as I attempted to walk on them and the incoming rippling waves were coming in quickly with the tide! It was not particularly easy to focus on the log in front of me, while all the while I was carefully looking at the vines above me. Was that an anaconda or just a long dripping vine? Surely the piranhas were gathering below the logs just waiting to munch on me. I may or may not have told Rick, "If I die having been eaten as a snake lunch, I will make sure that our church stops sending support to you."

Finally, after what seemed like miles, we reached land. (If I recall correctly, Rick said it was approximately 1/4 mile but it surely seemed much longer.) We continued our walk on land to see this ominous, old woman witch doctor. I am sure that I was a sight… wet clothes, stringy wet hair, and any semblance of mascara had long since been washed away, or worse yet, streaked down my face.

We arrived, I wished I had a camera! The village was remarkable. Having lived in rural Africa for many years, I should have been prepared, but nothing had prepared me for the sites we saw. We approached the outdoor living room or meeting place. It was made with tall poles and a grass roof. There were big tree stumps around the circumference for us to sit on. However, the site that made me almost giggle out loud was a HUGE pig lying in the middle of this living area. I guess one could liken it to a home that had a bear rug in front of the fireplace, except this was a large pig that was snoring. On the pig sat three roosters, all nestled together, sleeping and ignoring the rain around them.

We sat for a little while talking to the one man who was sitting there, and shortly, we were joined by Doña Coraçao. She carried a lovely tray, filled with depression-glass cups and saucers. How incongruous! In almost primitive surrounding, she had a beautiful set of dishes. The pink of the cups was in sharp contrast to the gray wet skies and surrounding area. The steam from the hot tea was such a welcome sight for my chilled body. I could not have been more content sitting on a fine Edwardian sofa having tea with the Queen.

The most riveting thing to me, however, was Doña Coraçao's face. I was expecting anger, harshness and disdain. But what I saw was completely different. True, her face was aged, and her hair was white, and the wrinkles from her life in the harsh Brazilian heat were very deep and pronounced. But there was a softness in her eyes that I was not expecting. Her dark, parchment-like skin almost glowed. She was pleasant and cordial and had a gift for hospitality. Her smile was warm and welcoming. I had not expected this.

Doña Coraçao

After serving us tea, and having conversation with Rick, Doña Coraçao proceeded to unceremoniously bump the pig out of the way. The roosters flew off with disgruntled annoyance at their nap being disturbed. Another treat was being prepared for us. Acai is a purple berry, found mainly in South America. The palm trees where they grow are very tall. Someone had climbed those trees to bring down the dark purple berries to serve their guests. There was a large flat stone near where we were sitting, and Doña Coraçao got down on her knees and started grinding those berries with her hands, until the dark purple juice ran down the trough that had been chiseled in the large flat rock and then into a bowl. The juice was brought into the house and laced with sugar and we were served this refreshing, sweet nectar. I can remember eyeing Doña Coraçao as she pressed the berries; she had a glow on her face. She was not at all what I had pictured. She was tender, and her face was soft and attractive.

We needed to say our goodbyes before the night came upon us so that we could get back home before dark. I hugged Doña Coraçao as we left, and she returned a warm hug. The glow of her face was imprinted on my mind. We had just walked a few hundred yards out of her village when I asked Rick to ask the girls to give a report of their time that weekend. With joy on their faces, the two students shared with enthusiasm that Doña Coraçao had decided to give her life to God that weekend.

That was the reason for the GLOW! That was the reason for the JOY! The bitterness and resentment of those who had not been Christ followers was replaced by the joy of being forgiven and becoming a child of God. Tears filled my eyes as Rick was sharing with me what the girls told him.

The walk back to the boat was a breeze. I think that I was the one floating, not the logs, as this time I traversed them with ease. I had no thoughts of snakes, but only of the sweet glowing face of this former witch doctor. We later heard that Dona Corazon became a witness for God in that river community, and many of her family came to trust and put their faith in God. That day is a precious memory as I saw the fruit of Kim's and Rick's labor.

21

I Can See Clearly Now

God so often had surprises in store for us when we visited other countries; our second trip to China was no exception. In 2001, my husband Lynn and I were traveling with Don, the senior pastor of our church and his wife Donna to a large city a few hours outside of Beijing. On the long bus ride, Donna and I were chatting and laughing a lot, when all of a sudden, I saw what looked like a neon green worm making its way across my left eye. Slightly startled, but trying to remain composed, I calmly asked Donna, "Do you see a small, green worm in my eye?"

Giving me a quizzical look, she slowly replied, "No, I don't see anything," and she probably began to wonder if I was experiencing some strange, hallucinogenic form of jet lag.

I ignored the "worm" as we continued our journey. Checking in at the hotel was a lengthy process. As Donna and I continued our banter back and forth, my left eye went completely blind with what looked like a shower of blood. It appeared as if someone had thrown a bucket of red paint inside my eye making the left eye totally blind. I didn't want to alarm anyone until I could figure out what was going on. As we entered the elevator, I kept closing my eyes, thinking when I opened them, the left eye would be clear and my sight restored. But alas, when I closed my right eye, I was in fact, blind in the left eye.

As soon as we got into our hotel room, I asked Lynn if he could see any blood in my eye, and just like Donna, he calmly said he saw nothing; no blood at all. We actually were scheduled to be at a meeting that night, and it was quite surreal to try and act completely normal, knowing that something serious had happened to my left eye. After the meeting was concluded we asked Joe, the man that we were visiting, if there were any eye doctors in the city. He said he would check for us. He found the name of a lady optometrist; we planned to visit the next day.

The visit was not particularly reassuring. When I entered the little office, she asked me to lie down on the table. The "white" sheet on the table looked as though it had been very well used by many people. She had a little "maybe it was white once" linen cloth with a hole cut in the very center that looked as well used as the sheet. Internally I asked God if we could please skip the part where she covered my face with that cloth, and to my deep relief, it was set aside and she just examined my eye. Her conclusion: my retina had almost completely detached. She then went on to say that she had a procedure that would fix it for only $20 US dollars. That sounded like quite the bargain to have my sight restored, however Joe felt it might be a good idea to get a second opinion. He made some calls and found an excellent eye clinic back in Beijing.

The appointment was made for the next morning, and Joe hired a taxi to take us on the three-hour trip back to Beijing. The eye clinic was immaculate and completely professional. The first sweet, older lady doctor that examined me advised that she could make me a special cup of Chinese tea that would fix the problem. But then another doctor came in to examine me. He was not sure the tea would help, and decided to call in the doctor who was the head of the Eye Clinic. I began to be slightly amused as our already tiny waiting room became more crowded: the older lady doctor, the second doctor, the head doctor, a nurse, Joe, Lynn, and another man whom I did not recognize. After chatting a few minutes, the head doctor asked for someone to turn off the overhead light. Someone stood and obliged. I later asked Lynn who that was, and he chuckled and said, "The taxi driver!" After the three-hour ride to Beijing, he was eager to hear what the doctor had prescribed, so he decided to come into the examining room as well. (There were always things to put a smile on your face.) The head doctor determined that I should not fly back to the states with the retina hanging on, literally by a thread; he advised surgery for the next day.

We found a little guest house there in Beijing, and I settled in for a much-needed sleep. Lynn decided he would like to have a second opinion with our US doctor, Dr. Terry. With the 12-hour time difference, it was fine to call him late that night. Lynn walked to a local market and found a man who had a little stall, with a bright red telephone that he allowed people to use to make calls, for a fee, of course. Lynn got connected with Dr. Terry, and he suggested that he would call a retina specialist that he knew, Dr. Rankin in Greensboro, North Carolina.

Lynn contacted him with another long-distance call. Lynn gave Dr. Rankin the details of what was happening. He asked Lynn the name of the Beijing eye surgeon. There was a little pause on the line. Dr. Rankin had gone to medical school with the surgeon at Harvard! Lynn was stunned, and Dr. Rankin went on to say he would call the surgeon and have a chat about my case! Thank you, God! You never make mistakes! What an amazing God moment.

A fun fact: my surgery was scheduled for 7:00 AM Friday, and I found out later that our church had called a special prayer meeting for me at 7:00 PM Thursday evening, the exact time when I was being operated on. What a precious, faith-building time.

We arrived at the hospital early. After I was prepped, they told me I could go say good-bye to my husband in the waiting room. Our dear friend Joe stayed with Lynn the whole time. When I went out to see them (but not necessarily to say good-bye), Joe lightened the mood as he always could. "Judy, should I go out while you are in surgery and find a seeing eye dog for you just in case this doesn't work?" Laughter is such good medicine and we appreciated Joe's humor that morning!

The surgery was completed successfully, and I was sent off with a big patch of gauze and tape over my left eye. The blindness continued for about 6 weeks, but the adventures that God had planned for our trip were just beginning.

The Monday after surgery, we were scheduled to visit the famous Great Wall of China. The family that we were visiting asked if it would be okay for a young, female university student to accompany us to the Great Wall because their daughter had a basketball game they wanted to attend. We agreed, and what a special time we had with her. Chinese people are extremely tender and sensitive to older folk, especially if one is half blind! The young student was an amazing guide as we visited this historic site for the first time. She shared with us that construction on the Great Wall began 770 years before Christ was born and was completed in 221 BC. What an amazing history!

Little did we know that in this new connection at the Great Wall, God was threading His tapestry needle, but it would be revealed later just how the threads were being woven together. Our lovely, young guide, let's call her Mary for her protection, was such a dear! She held my arm gently yet firmly as we climbed the Wall. She was so careful with me; she knew that seeing with only one eye was affecting my depth perception, and she didn't want me to miss a step. We talked all the way up to the crest of the Wall, and I asked her to share her story with me–was there anything that I could be praying about for her. She shared much of her background and then began to share a touching story of, "William," the young man with whom she had fallen in love.

He was a music major with a vision to start a school of worship that would teach young house church believers how to lead worship, how to play a keyboard, and how to write songs of worship. However, Mary's mother did not approve of their getting married because Mary's family were Han, the most traditional of Chinese families, and her boyfriend was from a minority group. Mary's prayer request was that her mom's heart might soften towards William. We stood on the top of the Wall and prayed together about her future. Lynn took our photo—me with my eye patched and both of us with the biggest smiles.

Our tour of the great wall

The following Monday we were to meet up with Don and Donna at the Forbidden City. They gave us the news that the son of dear friends of ours back in the States had taken his life that morning. Our hearts were broken because we had been praying with our friends for the son's life for several months. They asked if Lynn could do his funeral the day after we arrived home. When we returned with Don and Donna two days later, we were able to be there for the young man's funeral.

22
China Focus

When we started the China focus at our home church in 2001, Lynn had contacted the House Church Uncles in China to ask how our church could be of help without interfering or messing up what the Chinese believers were already doing. The house church movement in China was growing at a rapid rate. As Americans, we didn't want to suggest a different path when they were already doing it so well. The response of the House Church Uncles: "We need people to disciple our new believers. Many of them are heading out as global workers after hearing only about ten messages."

Their plan, which could utilize the gifts of an American church, was unique: they asked that we come to the city of their choosing and live together in a little, three- bedroom apartment with 15 Chinese young people, an interpreter, and a cook for a month at a time. The idea was to be in hiding from the police, as it was illegal for Christians to meet. We would not leave the apartment at all, except for an overnight each Saturday. Lynn and I would do a tourist thing or visit another city just to get out. This was certainly not a new concept for Chinese people, but for us it was very "out of the box." Regardless, we agreed to their request, and thus began a new and deeply faith-building chapter of our lives in ministry for Jesus.

The city we flew into was on the opposite side of China from the capital city of Beijing. The night before we entered our one-month experience, we planned to have dinner with one of the house church men. We were staying overnight at a hotel, and while chatting with him, there came a knock on our hotel door. A young man entered and our friend introduced us to him as William. Shortly after the introductions, William began to share his story, and our friend translated for us. He had traveled three days by train to meet us; he wanted to share his vision for the house church movement. William explained that he wanted to start a school for worship in which he would teach the worship leaders to play keyboard, to write songs, and to lead worship. Immediately Mary, our guide at the Great Wall, came into my mind's eye. It was almost verbatim what she had shared with me the previous month when she was talking about "her William."

When he finished sharing, I asked if he was dating a girl named "Mary." Slightly stunned, he responded yes and asked how I would know that. I walked over to the bedside table, picked up my Bible, and pulled out the photo of Mary and me that Lynn had taken at the Great Wall. I handed the photo to him for confirmation, and told him that Mary and I had prayed for him that day and that I promised her I would continue to pray for both of them. That's why I had our photo in my Bible. Needless to say, we were both awestruck.

William and Mary

The exquisite hand of our Sovereign God weaves together the threads of our lives into His tapestry. The family we were with in Beijing did not know anything about William, and the Chinese House Church Uncle that we were with in Kunming did not know anything about Mary. Yet here we were, thousands of miles apart, and God allowed us to meet both of them! Again, to say we were amazed by this Divine Appointment would be an understatement. A seed of anticipation started to grow as we wondered what God was planning. That connection helped us and our home church to connect with them, and allowed our church to come alongside to buy instruments for the fledgling school of worship. And with God directing the plans, and His Spirit to inspire hearts and minds, the school grew to a substantial size, blessing the House Churches, and blessing us as we watched God's hand at work.

After that special God-time with William, we started our month-long assignment of teaching. Lynn had done some research and found an amazing study called Firm Foundations. It was a study put together by New Tribes Missions. It was excellent: 52 lessons from Creation to Christ, touching the highlights of redemption and God's plans for us. It was especially wonderful that we could find it in both English and Mandarin. We were able to give each of the 15 students their own copy in Mandarin, but Lynn could teach in English.

The tiny apartment was a buzz of activity when we entered that first night. The students had been chosen from many house churches in different parts of China. They had unpacked their meager belongings and were settling in. All the curtains had been drawn, and some of them were busy making little 'socks' out of old jeans to cover the chair legs so that when we were in class the sound of moving chairs would not be heard from down below. All of the female students were in one room, and all of the male students were in another. Lynn and I occupied the third bedroom. Our beds were interesting in that neither one had a mattress. Lynn had a long wooden door, and I had a shorter wooden door, and we both had a pillow and a sheet. Needless to say, it took some getting used to.

All of the students spoke Mandarin, but we did not know a word. In many ways it was just a cacophony of unrecognizable sounds to us. Lynn and I both had studied Romance languages, so there were some sounds and words that were understandable whether Italian, French, or Spanish, but in Mandarin, there was absolutely nothing that we could pick up. (This was in the early 2000's so there was no Google Translate to help us communicate.) We had been told by the House Church leaders that some of the students also really wanted to learn English and that there were several who could speak limited English. In preparation for English as a Second Language teaching, we brought along Scrabble and other word games to play with them in the evenings. While Lynn studied and prepared the lessons in our bedroom, I was out in the living room, attempting to make new friendships with these young people with whom we would live for the next month - using board games to have a little fun while helping them learn to read and speak more English.

On our very first evening there, while Lynn was in the bedroom studying, and I was attempting to make conversation, there came a knock at the front door. A sweet, glowing Chinese lady entered the living room. "Elizabeth" was a friend of one of our students, and she had come by so that we could pray with her. Her house church had recently collected enough money to buy two, one-way tickets for her and her husband to go to Myanmar to be missionaries. Fascinated by her story, I went to our bedroom to ask Lynn to come out and pray for her.

What a sweet, God-filled moment it was as we prayed for her and her husband, knowing that she was starting on this journey to a land that she had never visited to tell people who spoke a different language about Jesus. When Lynn finished praying, he went back to study, and Elizabeth began to share a little bit more of her story, while Peter, one of the students, interpreted for me.

Elizabeth began by apologizing to me for not kneeling when the pastor prayed. Peter explained that it was their custom to kneel when someone was praying over you. As Peter interpreted, she shared her story with me. She and her husband were house church pastors. One day as they were preaching about Jesus, the police burst into their little house church and arrested them. They were put in jail for three years; they were completely separated, unable to see one another, and they were treated very poorly. When they were finally released from prison, and were back into their home, their zeal to share the liberating freedom of Jesus Christ had them preaching the Gospel again.

It was only a matter of months before the police arrived at their home and they were imprisoned this time for 18 months. When they were released, they went back to their home, and soon they were back preaching the Word of God. A third time the house was invaded, but the people of the church heard the police coming and sent Elizabeth and her husband running out the back door. They tried to get them to escape by climbing a wall, but before they could scale it, the police pulled Elizabeth down, and in doing so broke both of her legs. They were taken to prison again, this time to stay 2 years. Elizabeth was never given medical attention to fix her legs, so they both healed crookedly.

When they were released, Elizabeth was able to go to the hospital to have her legs broken and reset properly, but as a result, there was very little movement from her legs. As she lifted the skirt of her dress to show me, I did my best to hide how broken-hearted I was as I looked at the railroad track-like scars that ran up both of her legs. She explained, "I can no longer bend my legs properly. I cannot kneel; I am sorry I stood to be prayed over."

Deep empathy gripped my heart for Elizabeth, and with tears streaming down my cheeks, I prayed for her again, this time with a much greater awareness of the sacrifices she had made in her life to follow Jesus. Yet, even today, I can still see the joy on her face as she shared that they had been chosen to be given the one-way tickets to start a new life in a country to which she had never been, to learn a language she had never heard, so that they could share Jesus with the people of Myanmar.

Within those first few hours in the apartment, it seemed like we had a situation that was going to be impossible. Hide out in an apartment with 15 students, a translator, and a cook for a whole month? When Elizabeth left, I went into the bedroom and shared with Lynn, "This is going to be the hardest month of our life. I am glad that we came first before bringing others from our church to experience this."

Interestingly, that was the only fleeting moment that we felt we'd made a mistake! The next morning, we awoke with the sound of people worshipping quietly and praying. I peeked out of our bedroom door and saw all 17 of them kneeling on the tiled floor, upright and straight as arrows, beseeching God for His blessing. They were praying for those being persecuted; asking for Grace for those who were imprisoned (which included the parents of two of our students, Paul and Anna, from different cities). One evening they asked us if we could teach them how to respond when they are imprisoned. We asked for His guidance to know how to answer them.

With the curtains drawn, we never knew what the weather was outside in the weeks we lived there, but we knew it was cold and there was no hot water. The apartment's water heaters were shut off on March 15, and it was early April, so each morning Lynn and I woke to take very cold showers. On the upside, it woke us up pretty quickly. However, I started to notice that all of the girls would come out of their rooms with wet hair before supper. About three weeks in to our month, it occurred to me to ask why they all showered in the afternoon. The building had a solar heater; if we had showered in the evening, the water would have been at least warm from the sun. We had so much to learn.

Sometimes Lynn and I joined their 5:00 AM prayer meetings. We couldn't understand the words, but we could easily understand their feelings. When we did come out to join them, they would find pillows for us to kneel on. They understood our enthusiasm to be part of their prayer time didn't come with their hard-core discipline of kneeling on hard tile for an hour without wiggling around! It was quite humbling.

Early morning prayer time

The month went by so quickly, and what a month that was! The students were like sponges; they wanted to soak up all the knowledge they could from the Word. They wanted to understand it, absorb it, and apply it. We loved them so much; it was like breathing--a natural, effortless response. They inspired us as they were being inspired by the Living Word. On Saturday nights we would all slip out, two by two at different time intervals, and come back together on Sunday night. Lynn and I actually began to miss them in the 24 hours we were apart.

When we tried to play games in the evening to practice English, the students came up with a better way: they asked us to correct their pronunciation as they read Bible verses. Over and over, we would do that. You would think that we would have all those chapters of Scripture memorized!

All month long we had rice for every meal, usually with a boiled vegetable of some kind with it. The students were from very poor villages, so meat, or chicken would have been too expensive. We occasionally had peanuts with the rice or scrambled eggs, but never meat. (We became quite proficient in using chopsticks and it was a big celebration when Lynn learned to eat the peanuts with them.)

Being culturally inept, we had to learn some difficult lessons. One weekend Lynn and I came back earlier than the others and two of the girls had a special treat prepared for us: Fish heads. Not the body... just the head, with the shiny eyes staring at us. We told the girls we loved them so much that we would share the eyes and the cheeks with them!

Lynn and I talked about doing something special for everyone when we came back together on Sunday nights. We found a place to order pizza, and ordered three. We also ordered a big, creamy birthday cake for Ruth to celebrate her turning 20. Two of the boys went to the store to pick up the special treats. As we came back together that night, we sang songs, and played pin-the-tail on a donkey that Lynn had drawn. It was a hilarious evening and we had so much fun. The Chinese culture is quite homogenous, and they would not want someone shamed, so as each one of us was blindfolded, all the others would shout out hints to tell them which way to go or take them by the hand to pin the tail exactly. We wound up with 17 tails all in the exact same spot on the donkey.

Things were going great until the pizza and the cake showed up. They all looked at the pizza, but immediately dug into the big cream cake. The pizza was avoided. We thought that it was only because it was something new, similar to our reaction of being served a fish head. Later they shared that the money that we spent on that pizza was more than they would make in a month. To them, eating it did not feel right: unlike an American delicacy, it was more like an exorbitant amount of money. We learned a hard cultural lesson by the mistake on our part, but we were graciously forgiven.

The apartment had a water cooler. The beverage of choice for the whole month was cool water or lukewarm water. I remember sitting one evening with the students studying all around us, huddled over their Bibles. Lynn and I were reading and sipping our warm water, and we contentedly smiled at one another. "This feels a little like being at Starbucks back home." We were so at peace and felt totally enamored with these absolutely wonderful, on-fire-for-Jesus, young people.

***

It was never far from anyone's mind that it was illegal for all of them to be gathered together to study the Bible. They were very much aware that, if found by the police, Lynn and I would be sent back to the US, but they would be imprisoned. Hence, we were very careful with loud singing, and we never all left at the same time on Saturdays. One night, when we were sitting and reading Scripture, there was the dreaded knock on the door. Anna, whose parents were both in prison, went to the door to look through the peak hole. It was the police. She closed the peep hole and motioned for all of us to go to our rooms, which we did with unbelievable quietness. Lynn and I lay down on our "doors", fully clothed; we hardly breathed. Surprisingly, the police did not come in, but stood in the doorway asking our sweet, brave, diminutive Anna her name and where she was from. They asked if there were any other people living here? "Yes." she responded, and she named three people.

The interrogation took almost an hour. There was not a sound anywhere in the apartment. There were no bathroom visits or teeth brushed that night as she stood answering questions. Instead, each of us in the three rooms sent prayers Heavenward to the Father for the protection of the 17 young souls desperate to serve Him. One of the treasures that I still have is a book of prayers, journaled every day we were in China, by a dear friend named Shirley. When we returned to the United States, she met us at the airport and handed me her prayer journal. So precious were the prayers that she prayed on our behalf and that of the students. One of her morning prayers gave me chills. I checked the date and compared it to my own journal. Shirley prayed, "Father, I particularly pray for Lynn, Judy, and the students, that they might be surrounded by your angels. I pray that the police will not find them, nor imprison any of the students. Blind the eyes and close the ears of anyone who would cause them harm." *The same morning that she prayed was the very night that the police visited us.* (It was her morning - our night.) The eyes of the police were blinded; their ears kept from hearing our whispered prayers.

It's not hard to understand that by the end of our month together, we all felt like family. A plan had already been set in place where two others from our church were coming to teach the next month, so the time was nearing when we would say goodbye. God laid it very clearly on our hearts that we wanted us to have a foot washing and communion the night before we left.

Crying and showing emotion is not a natural response in the Asian culture, but that night, as 17 young people sat in a circle with Lynn washing and me drying their feet, their tears flowed and ours did too. It was a strange experience for them culturally, as well; it was not natural for "old people" to be bent over washing the feet of younger ones. We all knew we probably would never see one another again.

The Scripture reminds us, "How beautiful are the feet of those who bring good news!" Our lives were so greatly impacted by our time in China: God faithfully supplying an eye surgeon to repair my damaged retina; a beautiful girl named Mary, who lived in Beijing and asked us to pray for her Mom to approve her marriage to a young Music major who wanted to start a School of Worship; a chance meeting weeks later with that same boyfriend thousands of miles across the country, identifying his girlfriend Mary by her photo with me at the top of the Great Wall; praying for Elizabeth and her husband as they started toward the mission-field in Myanmar; and the lifelong blessing of our time with these 17 absolutely amazing young people!

We left China forever changed by the dedication of those young people who, we believe, are someplace around the world right at this very moment telling people about the Jesus whom they serve so faithfully. Our eyes were opened to so many things— mine, physically and both of ours, spiritually. All for His Glory! All for His Kingdom to come!

23

Meeting Mikel
Albania and Kosovo

The war in Kosovo and the affects that spilled over into its neighbor Albania had been in the news just months before our first scheduled trip to visit partners scattered around Europe. We did not feel that things were so bad that we should cancel our scheduled pastoral visits, so we carried on with our plans.

Albania had seen a great change in the decade of the 1990's. First, it removed itself from the Communist Party and that was a huge change for the people. They were mostly happy about the decision, but it brought many disruptions. We talked to a family there who said that under communism, they were responsible for their own home and property; but outside their gates, the communists were responsible for keeping the streets clean. So, people carried on with their usual lifestyle, but now there was no one to take care of the outside, and trash piled up. No one would take responsibility.

There was an attempt at the ethnic cleansing of all Albanians. It was spear-headed by Yugoslavia and Serbia. About 92% of the population of Kosovo, approximately 1.8 million, were Albanians living in Kosovo, and almost a million fled to Albania after seeing what was happening as this "cleansing" continued and hundreds of thousands were killed. Adding almost a million people to the western borders of a country certainly changed things. People were crowded into tents and every other place they could find to stay. Food was not sufficient nor easily found. Albania used to be part of the Ottoman Empire, so there was a distinct presence of Muslims. It became a communist country in 1991, so religious activities had been eradicated. Albania contained quite a mixture of beliefs, but mostly it became known as an atheistic country.

The genocide in Kosovo was horrific. Armed forces from Yugoslavia and Serbia had come in, determined to rid the country of all Kosovo Albanians. They went from village to village hunting down the men and teen-aged boys, killing them and dumping their bodies into open graves. Just before we arrived in Albania, NATO forces had intervened in Kosovo, called a cease-fire, and driven out most of the warring factions. Many of the people who had fled to Albania returned to their homes in Kosovo, leaving behind mountains of plastic bags and trash.

Our plane landed in Albania several hours later than was scheduled. We knew that the partners we were visiting would not be available to meet us because there was a graduation in the school where they were working. We were not sure who was picking us up, but they assured us that someone would be there at the airport.

It was an exceptionally hot day when we arrived. Inside the small airport, it was surprising to see so many men with faces covered in ski masks, holding weapons aimed at the passengers disembarking the plane. Passport control went fairly smoothly, and we walked to the exit. A man held up our name on a sheet of paper, and we met Mikel, an Albanian who made his living as a driver. He was cordial and accommodating, despite his long wait for us. His face was red and quite sunburned from standing outside in the hot sun while we were delayed. His English was extremely limited, but he conveyed to us that he was taking us to a restaurant by the Adriatic Sea because our hosts were going to be busy for a while longer. Mikel's English was much better than our Albanian. He ordered us dinner, and we stayed at the little restaurant for a few hours, until Mikel received a phone call that we could come to the school.

It was almost midnight by the time we arrived, and our hosts were tired from a full day, as ready for bed as were we. They told us that plans had changed. They needed to go to Kosovo to meet with their team, so we would be leaving the next morning at 4 AM to drive to Pristina, the capital of Kosovo. Flexibility is always the name of the game when traveling. They directed us to one of the college dormatory rooms where we would catch a few hours' sleep before leaving. We didn't bother opening suitcases since we were leaving in just four hours. We lay down on the bunk beds, slept in our clothes, and were ready to leave four hours later.

The drive through Albania was interesting. Albania's brutal leader for 40 years, Enver Hoxha, feared invasion from neighboring countries, so from 1960-1980, he built bunkers all over the country for protection. There are two million people and over 700,000 bunkers, but these small cement shelters were never used for war. Construction of these bunkers helped make Albania one of the poorest countries in Europe as it is today.

The mountain range was quite beautiful. The official name of the range was The Albanian Alps, but it was locally known as the Accursed Mountains because folklore said they were haunted. The 13-hour trip was long but fascinating. There were several road blocks along the way, again with men in ski masks but no-one trying to make trouble for us.

The drive through Kosovo was eye-opening. Eight out of ten houses were burned to the ground, and entire villages had been destroyed by the ethnic Serbs. My heart broke as we passed village after village—totally devastated. There were mass open graves and many bombed-out bridges that NATO had destroyed to deter the outside armies. We reached Pristina well after dark and stayed in a guest house that was lit with lamps and candles rather than electricity. Several other families gathered there but we didn't stay up to talk too long. Bed felt good!

Several times during the night we were awakened as the unmistakable sound of Huey helicopters circled the area where we were staying. It was strange how just the sound of those whirling helicopter blades quickly took us back to our days of the conflict in Zimbabwe. Those helicopters, flying low over our house, were either carrying the wounded to the hospital or headed to the morgue with body bags hanging on the outside.

There were 38,000 troops in Pristina, from all of the countries represented by NATO, and the city was overcrowded by tanks and army vehicles filling the streets. We spent a few days there. Several of the workers we visited were discouraged and tired, and we had many opportunities to listen to their stories. We heard many gruesome tales of murders and atrocities that had been taking place during that time of ethnic cleansing. Lynn prayed with several people and gave them encouragement from God's word.

It is easy to get weary from the work in a war-torn country. Our hearts were touched and moved with compassion. We met a man named Cary, who was there evaluating how teams could come in to help in the villages where all of the houses had been burnt to the ground. With the adult men all killed there was no one to help with any rebuilding. Cary put the challenge to Lynn: Could you gather a team from your church to come back and help? After hearing more details, Lynn agreed that we would put together a team and send them as soon as possible after we returned to the U.S.

It was time for us to catch our plane back to Germany, but our flight left from Albania. Our hosts had decided that they were going to stay on in Kosovo because they had not been able to purchase the land they were looking for. They told us that they had asked Mikel, the same driver who picked us up at the airport, to drive us back to Albania.

We packed up and left to drive back to Albania the next morning. As I mentioned, Mikel didn't speak English, but he had one demo music CD in English. It was an old Shania Twain song,

"That Don't Impress Me Much" that he played on a loop for the entire drive back to Duress.

Mikel took a route back through Macedonia, thinking it would be safer for us. There were many more check-points and many more men in ski masks. We noticed exchanges of cigarettes between Mikel and the guards; that seemed to make our getting through the check-points a little easier. He stopped the car often to chat with people on the road to get the lay of the land. Mikel might have known a good portion of the 92% of the country who were Kosovo Albanians. Knowing that there were still Serbs there, I am sure it was a little harrowing for him. But there were also areas where he sped along as quickly as he could.

In one area we were slowed because of a street riot, and we were not sure what was happening. With the road blocked and several hundred people shouting in the street and coming down to where our little car was, we began sending up prayers. Mikel tried to speed through, but the crowd was too big. Miraculously, the rioting people stopped about four feet short of our car, then parted, and we drove through. We were convinced that our prayer partners back in the U.S. were praying for us that very minute. Later that evening back in Albania, we saw the report on the news that the grenades and shooting were again Serbs vs Kosovo. There were hundreds gathered until the NATO forces stepped in. Yet God's timing was perfect for us to drive through.

Our hosts had asked Mikel to drop us at a hotel in Duress when we arrived and then pick us up the following day to take us to our 3 PM flight. As we got closer to Durres, Mikel, in his very broken English, said, "You don't really want to stay in a strange hotel, do you?" He said he had a better plan. We stopped for dinner, with him insisting on paying for our meal. Then he drove us to his home where his wife, Emira, was waiting with an amazing Albanian dessert that she had prepared for us. The rest of the evening was spent meeting his two children and a long string of friends and relatives who stopped in for dessert, coffee, or fruit and to be introduced to his American friends.

Mikel and Emira proceeded to give us their bed, while they slept on the sofa, and their children went to relatives' homes. We were treated like royalty by a man we had met only as our driver. The next morning, after a tasty breakfast, he asked if he could show us the ancient ruins of Durres of which he was so proud. His friend, who was quite fluent in English, joined us and made communicating much easier. Through translation, Mikel shared that his son would like to go to medical school, and his daughter wanted to be a teacher. He told us that they needed to learn English to be able to do that. Mikel asked if we would consider coming back and holding an English camp for the children of Durres. We told him that we would like very much to do that and would try our best to do it someday.

Our morning in Duress was delightful! In the back of my mind, I tucked away the thought that somehow, someway, someday, I want to accomplish the goal of bringing back an English team. The goal got delayed when our mission focus was turned to China for three and a half years. But keeping my word has always been on my heart. What a surprising turn of events that God brought Mikel into our lives! We saw His fingerprints once again in an unexpected way.

24

Return to Kosovo

L ynn and I took to heart the request to return to Kosovo with a team to help do some rebuilding of homes. We contacted Cary, the local man who had made the request, and set up a date to go. We advertised at church for a team and had a wonderful response from people willing to venture into that war-torn county. I teased Lynn after he told me he could not get away from work to go back, but he said, "It would be a good idea for you to lead the team."

Landmines, tanks, and helicopters aside, we were sure the trip would be quite safe. I had a chat with our more curious team members, letting them know that I might have to put a leash on them. We were told not to let anyone go out walking by themselves where there was caution tape, because all of the land mines had not yet been picked up.

There were no direct flights to Kosovo at the time, so we flew to Austria, had a long layover, and then made our way to Pristina. One of the team remembers being shocked by the buildings in the capital. The ones that were still standing seem to have satellite dishes at every window. One building in particular was about 30 stories high and the top ten floors on one side were simply gone from the bombings. There was devastation everywhere. The men of the town–the dads and older brothers and uncles–had all been killed and were in the mass graves at the other end of the town.

After buying supplies in the capital, we drove to the town of Orlan that would be our home for two weeks. There were two dorm rooms with bunks; the girls stayed in one and boys stayed in the other. The team was joined by two groups from different parts of the USA, and we were amazed how well the teams worked together. After our first morning gathering, we were given assignments for the day by the project captain. Some were digging a new sewer system; some were doing construction; and some were putting speed bumps in the road to try to slow down the NATO tanks that would rumble through, not noticing the little children playing in the area. We were told that the town leaders would select which home should be rebuilt first. We rebuilt the home of an elderly couple whose home had been destroyed but who had been spared during the killings. The devastation was widespread, and the flat effects on faces told the story.

I am not very good at construction. Or following directions. Jack, an amazing male nurse, and I were instructed to whitewash the walls. The liquid was thin, like water. We were told to put five to seven coats of that liquid on all the walls. Jack was obedient. He started and was doing a great job. When I arrived after making the team breakfast and cleaning up, I thought surely, we didn't really need that many coats. I talked Jack into making our buckets of liquid much thicker so we could do more walls and save time. Poor Jack. We made ours nice and thick. At the end of about seven hours of working, we were not quite finished with our first coat of thick whitewashed walls. The next morning when assignments were given out, Cary, our leader, took me off whitewashing. I couldn't understand why until he showed everyone our house—just touch the walls and big chunks of whitewashed plaster fell off.

I became full-time cook and bottle washer! I was also assigned to make the trip to Pristina to buy supplies. No two things are bought in the same store. One store had nails. Several blocks away were paint brushes. Another four to five blocks away was whitewash. I got my steps in, but would rather have been with the team.

One of our guys, Dave, was assigned to empty all of the crates that had come in from all over the U.S. He developed a system to organize and separate the tools. Dave was shy but invaluable. One day we had piled into the van that had no seats. Sixteen of us were sitting on the metal floor. The team that had worked on the road bumps had done a great job. The bumps were big and sturdy and came up unexpectedly. Dave was balancing himself on the ledge by the back doors when Cary hit a bump much too fast. As if we were watching in slow motion, the back doors flung open, and Dave, who was leaning on them, flipped backwards out of the van. "Dddddaaaaavvvvveeeeee!" we all shouted in unison as we saw him disappear out the back. He was pretty scratched up but was such a great sport. Dave became the center of all of our concern for the following few days.

As much as we wanted to see the homes completed, our hearts were drawn to the children–some of whom were quite shell-shocked. When we finished each hard day's work, we went out to play with the kids, teach them some English, and learn some Albanian. Our desire to share Jesus's Love in words fell short, but showing His love by our actions seemed to work.

The time went quickly. Our bodies were tired, and we were eager to get home to be with family. For the flight home we had to overnight in Switzerland. The extroverts among us were glad to have one more night with a group, but the introverts, having lived in very tight quarters for almost two weeks, were ready to have their own space. We enjoyed the night in Switzerland and then back to the airport for that last long flight home. As we were nearing Chicago, flying in over Canada, I noticed on the little map on the screen that the plane, which had been heading south over Lake Michigan had made U-turn; we were heading back to Canada. One of our team members was a commercial pilot, and I was sitting next to him. I asked what he thought it meant, and he replied that there must be bad weather in Chicago if we were going back to Canada. We disembarked in Toronto and stayed in another airport hotel. There was no customs officer there, so we could not get suitcases or clothes. The next day we went back to the airport and hopped a plane to Chicago, thinking that we would connect there to our North Carolina flights. However, when we arrived at O'Hare, all the people who had not gotten out the day before were trying to get on the available flights. Try as I might to find seats for us, there were none available. Another night in a hotel! The added nights were a little challenging for the group.

As I reflect on that trip with that team, I realize I learned so much. We all learned so much. Serving across cultures in a country so devastated by war opened our eyes to needs that some had never imagined. Jesus said to go out to all the world and make disciples. People can't know His Word if someone doesn't tell them or know His Love if someone doesn't show them. We raised our hands, saying, "Here am I, Lord; send me." We were blessed by the experience.

The Kosovo Team

25

An Open Door Set Before You Banda Ache

The three-year focus on China, the first part of our church's ten-year vision, was coming to an end. What a delight that over 200 people from the church had gone to serve in some way in China. The goal had been to educate and motivate the people of our church to the opportunities for sharing the Gospel in China, and they had taken up the challenge in some amazing opportunities.

The next three-year focus was to be on the Muslim world. In December 2004, Lynn went to a Conference that was focusing on Indonesia, the largest of the Muslim nations. Opportunities in many of those countries were closing to outsiders. If that were so, it would certainly impact our three-year focus. We didn't have too many connections in the countries where Islam was the major religion.

However, God had a different plan that He was going to reveal in His time, and that time was closer than we realized. On December 26, 2004, tragedy struck in Banda Ache, Indonesia with an underground earthquake off the Sumatra coast that affected the Indian Ocean. It caused a tsunami that impacted the coastal areas of Indonesia, Thailand, Sri Lanka, India, and the Maldives. The waves in many areas reached 30 feet in height. The epicenter was in Banda Ache where the waves reached 65 feet high and lasted about seven hours. The death toll in the combination of countries was about 225, 000 people, with 167,000 of them in Banda Ache, Indonesia alone. Scientists say that the energy that was produced from that earthquake would be like that of 23,000 atomic bombs.

Early in the morning of December 29, I heard my computer ding, indicating a new email. I am a very early riser and I went to the computer to see what was happening. A message had come in asking me if I thought that Lynn would be willing to go and help with pastoral opportunities in the wake of the tsunami. Sumatra, the hardest hit was under Sharia law. Shortly after the tsunami hit, they were not willing to allow outsiders from the west to come and offer support. There was devastation all over and the call came from a man from Georgia who was headed to help in Sri Lanka. He had another ticket and asked if Lynn would accompany him. He would need to get a variety of shots and be ready to be at the airport by 6 PM that evening.

Lynn is not an early riser, and the man needed an answer pretty promptly so he could get the tickets and information in Lynn's name. We have continued our practice of early morning tea in bed from our days in Zimbabwe. I wanted to proceed slowly and not blurt out this request before he had time to wake up. Meanwhile, I was emailing back and forth, trying to get as many details as I could to present logically to my process-oriented husband. For better or worse, I jump to respond without knowing all the details, but Lynn is much more methodical.

We finished our tea and time of prayer together, and I needed to jump in and broach the subject. "Lynn, they need help with the tsunami. A man was given your name, and they have asked you to travel to Sri Lanka to help." Lynn had many questions. He of course already knew why because the devastation was playing constantly on every TV channel. He wondered how he could possibly be ready in less than ten hours, packing and getting to the CDC for necessary shots. (The injections would not be effective for almost a week after given.)

With the tiniest of nudges, we got him all his shots, had him packed, and he was at the airport by 6 PM to make the last plane out of Greensboro to Atlanta. He would meet with his traveling companion the next morning for a 6 AM flight to Singapore. One of our friends asked at the airport where Lynn would stay that night. Bob gave Lynn money for a hotel, and then he and several others prayed Lynn off.

I returned home to another email, asking that I pack some food for Lynn. Many of the store shelves in Sri Lanka had been wiped clean by panic buying. Sadly, he was already gone and once again entrusted into the hands of God.

It took two full days of flights and connections before they reached Columbo, Sri Lanka. They hired a driver to take them to the other side of the island where most of the devastation from the tsunami took place.

They first went to the fishing village where houses used to be and now there was just rubble. They stood on top of the cliff looking over the edge at the devastation. When the tsunami hit, fishing boats had been pushed up and left hanging on the cliff walls. The force of the water from the waves hitting the cliffs pushed sea water up through crevasses and wells above the cliffs where people lived. Now the wells were contaminated with sea water, so it was no longer palatable for drinking.

Lynn and his new friend went down to the beach that still had bodies washing ashore. As he was on the beach, he was watching people being interviewed by Diane Sawyer of CNN, and it was quite a surprise to all of us to be watching CNN and see Lynn amidst all that tragedy. Everyone was overwhelmed by the devastation and the need. There was a great need to get the wells emptied of the sea water so that fresh water could get back into the wells. The men found an old diesel engine water pump and began draining some of the wells.

As we had been told, there was no food on any of the shelves in the little stores, but Lynn did manage to find a few cans of sweetened condensed milk in one shop. Those cans of milk and the protein bars that his companion had brought along were what kept the two men with any nourishment for the five days they were there.

Most of their time was spent on the ridge of the cliff, walking from home to home seeing how they could help. They were there mainly doing a survey trip to see how others could come and help, but they couldn't leave without attempting to alleviate some of the problems the people were experiencing.

The men had tickets to return to the USA after the five days so that they could report back to their organizations. On their way back to the Singapore airport, they stayed at the home of one of the believers, and I was able to call Lynn. One of our partners, who lived in Jakarta, found out that Banda Ache, realizing the depth of devastation there, had agreed to allow outsiders to come in to assist. Aproximately 167,000 had died in Banda Ache alone. Lynn was asked if he could take a flight from Singapore to Sumatra to help evaluate how our church could be of help there.

Lynn was tired beyond words: physically and emotionally, but he agreed to lengthen his stay and go to Medan, Sumatra. He met up with our friend there, and they wanted to fly to Banda Ache, but the airports were not in use; the runways had been destroyed. There was a fleet of US ships off shore, so the only way in was by boat or helicopters.

No one wanted to drive them to the coast. It was night time, so it would mean driving through the night into an area that was controlled by Ache rebels who had check points along the road. They were fighting the Indonesian government because they wanted control of the area and continue to maintain Sharia law which is incredibly strict Islamic law. The civil war had been going on for years, and this was a dangerous place to be. Finally, a man with a taxi was offered enough money to make the trip worthwhile to him.

After driving through the night, the first thing that they noticed was the smell of decay and petroleum all mixed together. It was 12 days since the tsunami had changed the lives of people in Banda Ache. Almost all of the buildings were leveled to the ground; there were approximately 600 bodies a day being recovered. Several European rescue teams were there, carrying out body bags, loading them onto trucks, and putting them in open graves. Lynn remembers seeing people so traumatized by what they saw that they had total flat effect.

As Lynn walked around the streets, he came upon a little boy who was squatting and aimlessly stirring a pot that held a large black river crab. He was not responding to any questions, but was totally traumatized. A lady who knew the boy walked up to them and said that the boy had been sent to the store up on a hill. While he was gone, the wave hit and his entire family was washed away–every member.

There were three waves that came in succession. The first one, around 65 feet high came in, and as it began to go out, the second wave came in and like a scrub brush, just leveled houses. A mosque was five kilometers from the coast line, and the wave stopped right before it. All around there were fishing boats sitting on top of roofs. A large ship anchored off the coast had been providing electricity to the city, and it was carried three and a half kilometers into the city and landed on some of the larger buildings.

Lynn returned from those two weeks away with gunk in his lungs from breathing the smells of death and foul air; he had a bad case of bronchitis. Before he left Sumatra, he asked me to make an announcement at church: help is needed: who would be willing to go?

That Sunday morning, with the devastation on people's mind, I made a plea at church. Who is passport-ready? We wanted to take a team of five to six people there as soon as we could. We needed some with musical talents to lead worship. The Christian relief people that were already on the ground giving all they had were in need of spiritual encouragement. They longed for someone to lead them in worship, and to serve communion. That kind of surroundings drains everything from one. Kate and Chad had musical gifts; they came up to me immediately after the service and volunteered go. Paul and Philip came to talk to me: "We have passports, we can go and serve."

Lynn returned home, tired and not very healthy, with his lungs full, but we got him an antibiotic and a few nights' sleep, and he made the turn around. Together, we headed back to Banda Ache.

It seemed like not a lot of progress had been made in the week that Lynn was gone, although 500-600 bodies a day were still being picked up. The rescue teams were exhausted but still working so hard. A missionary who had served many years in Banda Ache had been asked to leave when Sharia law took over. She had been gone for about five years but still had friends living in Ache and offered help to her friend. We were brought to the friend's home. The water had come in her home about eight feet and then had drained, leaving around one and a half feet of heavy, wet sludge throughout her house. Our team of six were joined by a few other Americans who offered to help us with the project.

To respect our Muslim friends, we covered ourselves just like the women of Banda Ache did. We wore long dresses with long sleeves and had our heads covered, as Sharia law required. The temperatures were close to 100 degrees and we were shoveling mud, but God truly gave us the strength to complete the task set before us.

One of the Imams, from the mosque asked Lynn, "Why is it that the infidel will come to help and countries of our own faith have deserted us?" Scores of neighbors came and sat by the house and watched us, with the flat effect of shock on their faces. They were totally shell-shocked by what they had experienced. "How did you find Americans to come do this work?" the Imam asked.

About 30 of us were staying in the house that one of the groups had found. We all slept on the floor, and dropped into deep, exhausted sleep each night. Several earthquake after-shocks occurred while we were there, and everyone quickly got up from whatever we were doing and ran outside, wondering if the next earthquake was happening.

It was a blessing to be able to be alongside the bruised and battered Indonesians who had lost so much. The houses could be rebuilt, but almost everyone who remained had lost family members. It was also a privilege to come alongside those outsiders who were weary beyond words from bringing food and helping with homes and all that needed to be done. We shared worship and communion, using some raisins that we had soaked to make a juice.

Was our time worth it? Yes. The Imams asked about the faith we had that would make us leave our homes to come and help them. The doors that we had felt were slammed shut were ripped open and smashed down by a wave. Where before there had been no way outsiders could come in and share our faith in a God who loved us, now that door was pushed open and people actually wanted to hear about the God that we served.

That door stayed open for almost a year. Our church was able to send in five more teams of workers to help build homes, dig wells, and more importantly, to share God's love with a people who otherwise might never have heard about Him. God opens doors, indeed.

26

Colors, Tastes, and Hospitality
Afghanistan and Pakistan

It was customary for us to take our Senior Pastor, Don, and his wife, Donna, with us as we went to new areas so they could learn about the people group with whom we would focus for the three years. Pakistan, Afghanistan and United Arab Emirates were the next places that we visited together.

We were in Northern Pakistan to speak at a conference for workers, most of whom were doctors. We dressed in the lovely, colorful clothes, called Shalwar Kameez, the national dress of Pakistani women, which included beautiful scarfs to cover our heads. When shopping for our outfits, we sat on colorful silk pillows scattered around on the floor while bolts of silks and other fabrics were rolled out in front of us. Tea is often brought because this is not a quick shopping trip. Then we went to a tailor to be measured for the outfits. We picked them up the next day.

The Pakistani food is amazing. God certainly prepared Lynn and me for the traveling that we have had the privilege of doing in so many different cultures. We found early in our travels that food is one of the love languages of the people. To say we simply enjoyed the variety of foods we ate over the years would be putting it mildly. We loved it all (except maybe the fish heads in China).

One of my favorite outings in many countries was going to the local markets. The stalls are filled to the brim with more varieties of rice that I even knew existed; nor did I realize each one was to be eaten with certain meats or vegetables, like fine wine pairings. As we walked through the markets, there were huge burlap sacks filled to the brim with colorful, fragrant spices, dates, a variety of kinds of raisins, and things that I had never seen or tasted. Seeing the many colorful varieties as well as fragrances was such a feast for the senses.

When we left the market, we went to visit the hospital at which one of our partners worked. The doctors and nurses there earned the respect of the local authorities because of their good work and their faithfulness. They were allowed to stay in the country even though they did not hold the belief of the majority of people.

It was a great week, spending time with people who had dedicated their whole lives to serving others in a sometimes-challenging and not-always-safe country.

***

It was time to move to Afghanistan. We boarded a ten-seater plane at the Islamabad airport and were on our way. We saw the topography very quickly change drastically. The Spin Ghar mountain range formed a natural border between Pakistan and Afghanistan. It extended for about 100 miles from Peshawar, Pakistan through the Lowrah Valley in Afghanistan. The mountains were dry and seemed to go on endlessly. The flight was only an hour from Islamabad into Kabul, but it was a world away. In Kabul we had to go through passport control, and then we got back on the same plane to fly to Mazar Sharif, where we were met by our friend David and his driver.

Our first stop was to a wonderful Afghan restaurant and a new cultural lesson. The men eat in a room by themselves unless they have a family with a woman, and then there is a family room where women are allowed. That was where we ate. Of course, there were no western clothes to be seen, and we were happy that we were in our Pakistani garb with our heads covered so we didn't stand out quite so much.

The family room had lovely Persian carpets, and we had big cushions to lean on as we ate on the floor. Kabli Rice is one of the most delicious dishes we have eaten. It was served on a large silver tray that was about two and a half feet in circumference, piled high with rice cooked with carrots, raisins and garlic. The rice covered the shanks of lamb underneath. Lamb was always my birthday meal as I was growing up, so this felt like quite a celebration. The waiters kept us plied with hot, freshly cooked Naan-e afghani, the traditional bread made with wheat flour and water. The dough is stretched in a large oval and brushed with egg wash and then baked in a very hot tandoori oven. Some of the bread they brought us had warm butter spread on it and a variety of seeds sprinkled on top: sesame, nigella, caraway or poppy seeds. It is the national bread of Afghanistan, and for better or worse, I could eat my weight in that hot delicious bread. It is, like all breads, best when eaten hot from the oven. When we were more than full, we did a little shopping and headed on for a two-hour drive to the next city where our host and his wife and two daughters lived.

It is hard to describe the terrain. Everything was tan! All one could see along the roads was sand. You could drive for miles and see only adobe-sand-colored mud huts. Camels, goats, sheep, and donkeys roamed freely. People mostly rode camels; horses or donkeys carried loads of food and fruits. We said repeatedly through the journey that we felt like we had gone back about 2000 years in time. The women were all covered in burkas, but the people were so friendly to us as outsiders. Everything was new and fascinating, and the two-hour drive went quickly. Over and over, we saw acts of kindness by the people whom we met in the country.

Hospitality is a core value. When we visited their homes, we were treated like honored guests. One of the valuable lessons I learned was that hospitality is not the same as entertaining.

Often when Westerners entertain, we focus on matching dishes, a lovely set table, and perfect cooking. What I experienced was that they gave from all that they had. We met strangers, and they immediately invited us in for tea, to stay as long as we wanted, with no regard for anything else they had planned. We were invited to stay overnight in many countries. As a guest in their home, one is under their protection and treated quite royally. They are taught that if someone is a guest, you show the highest hospitality, even to your enemy. When you "drop in" they never seemed inconvenienced at all. In one home we visited, after we were served tea, we left with a purse, and walnuts, and corn on the cob–gifts from people who did not even know us! They were not wealthy, but they gave from whatever they had. They listened and asked about our family. It was a beautiful example of people caring for people. Cathy, our hostess, gave us burkas to wear while we were there so that we fit in and did not bring attention to ourselves.

There is not much to do for entertainment in their village, but they were so creative. One night we went out to the large sand dunes, and the little girls rolled in the sand as we would have done in the snow. We had a picnic out on the dunes and watched the sun set and the moon rise. Such simple things, but so meaningful.

Our time in their city observing their work went quickly, and it was time to drive back to Mazar Sharif, where we would again be picked up by the ten-seat plane. Our departure was rather spectacular. We boarded the plane and were ready for take-off when we were told we needed to get off the plane and wait in the small hanger off the runway. We had no idea why. It turns out that President Carzai, the president of Afghanistan, was taking off the same time as we were, so we waited inside until he boarded. As Carzai was to take off on his big military cargo jet, two small jets, called warthogs, took off shooting flares out of the plane so that should anyone nefarious be attempting to shoot down his plane, the flares would deflect the rockets. His was an interesting send-off. We stood on the tarmac not too far away.

Friends from Kabul met us when we landed, and we did some sight-seeing in the capital. We spent the evening in the city, where the electricity goes off at 6 PM. As were walking on Chicken Street, the main street, (like 5th Avenue in New York, except that it was completely dark), we heard a rumbling noise behind us. We realized that we were sharing the street with a very large Norwegian tanker. NATO forces were all over the city those days and many countries were represented with tanks, helicopters and army vehicles. After some shopping, our friends drove us to one of their favorite restaurants a little out of town. It was completely dark, and we were sure that it was already closed. Our host assured us that it was not; it was just dark because of no electricity. Having the city and restaurants all lit up made their homes and shops easy targets for attacks, so the whole capital went into darkness at nightfall. We enjoyed another amazing Afghan meal, all by candlelight, and had such a great last night in that unique country with very hospitable, amazing people. Praise God for differences; He created people, food, clothing, and cultures to be interestingly different.

27

A Fulfilled Promise in Albania

What a delight when, as a church, we started the focus on the Muslim world three years later. We had met a wonderful couple, Mark and Keta, who live in Kavaya, Albania, not far from where Mikel lives in Durres. The promise we had made to Mikel and his family four years before came immediately to mind. Possibly, we had found a way to fulfill that promise. We asked Mark and Keta their thoughts on doing an English camp in their town, and they were excited about the possibility.

We announced to our church that we would have a trip going to Kavaya to do an English camp. Although Lynn could not make the trip, the response from the congregation was gratifying. I was still in touch with Mikel, who used to call us on holidays, so when we told him we were bringing people to teach English, he was thrilled. His son was a pre-med student away at school, but he would allow his daughter to attend. I say allow because the town of Kavaya is Muslim. Mikel's family was not Muslim, so there was a question of safety in a very different culture. He said as long as we were going to be there, he would agree.

What an amazing team of people came forward to do this camp. A super young man named Mike agreed to co-lead the team with me. He was amazing with his interpersonal skills and love for God. Everyone on the team were capable and enthusiastic. Greg from Brazil was the youngest; he had just turned 16, and he asked if he could join us.

The team studied and prepared for several months prior to leaving. We learned about the country and the culture. During the preparation time we also learned about each other's personalities and what each would bring to the team. The team was a perfect fit for the task before us. After months of fund raising, preparing, and praying, we were ready to go.

***

We arrived at the camp ground and thought it perfect for our camp. It was located right on the beach of the Adriatic Sea. There were several little hotel rooms, each equipped with a little "squatty potty" toilet, something new for the Americans. There was a drizzle of a shower which was all we really needed. A big field was in the center area, and we were delighted that we could use it for soccer or volleyball. We quickly found out, though, that field had a fine layer of dirt on top, making it look just perfect for sports, but it was previously a dumping area. Everyone was out playing soccer when Greg got a deep gash in his foot from a chunk of broken glass. My first nursing duty! Upon closer inspection, we found that the whole field had broken bottles, shards of glass, bottle caps, tin cans, and other trash. Our first joint activity was to get our team and all the campers together and walk side-by-side to scour the field to remove all of the dangerous pieces of trash. It was somewhat of a bonding time and our first big experience with the campers.

There were not enough rooms for all the campers and our team, so the first night, the men put up tents. In the middle of the night, a storm came up across the sea, and the tents were blown down in no time. It was an inauspicious start. From the trash in the field, Greg's deep cut, and the blown-over tents, it was a little discouraging. However, our team devotional reading for that morning was about "Trials and things that cause us to Grow our faith in God." Our perspective changed! Lynn had sent along cards for me to open on different days during the time we were away. The card for that day had a picture of a little girl with an umbrella. The message was, "There will be rain in seasons, but God gives showers of blessing." We really felt His hugs and His presence in every detail.

While we had been training in the States, we prepared the team that we wouldn't be having team meetings on this short-term mission. Most of the local parents had allowed their children to come only if it were not a religious camp. We needed to honor their request. We arranged the schedule so that, during the day, there were always two counselors off for an hour, and we encouraged them to use that time for their own personal Bible reading, reflection and prayer. I had ordered a fabulous short-term-trip devotional called *"Walk as He Walked"* for each member of the team, and each day we found the writings apropos to what each of us was facing that day. Serving cross culturally in close quarters with people who are not family or chosen friends can sometimes bring up personality challenges. But we had no challenge so great that God didn't have an answer.

One of the best things we learned was to pray and talk to God throughout the day for each need that arose. Sitting in silent meditation for periods of time has its place, but there is nothing quite like an hour-by-hour conversation with God as we faced new challenges. Often two or three would gather and talk to God as if He were actually standing with us. It was a precious time of connection to our heavenly Father.

Gabrielle said one day, "One of the teens is asking questions about my faith in God. She said my life is different; I have joy. If she has more questions, I am going to send her to you, Judy." The next day, the same girl started talking to Gabrielle and asking more questions. I was not around, and Gabrielle was able to answer the questions with her Bible and God's help. What an enlightening moment for her to see that she didn't need a pastor's wife. God helped her to share what she believed.

The week of camp was great! God provided the right team members and the right personalities for every aspect of the week.

Our feelings ran deep for all the young people of the camp after only one week with them. Relationships were forged. The English classes went well. For most of the teens, this was their first exposure to classes with English speakers and to being with a group of Christian adults whose lives centered around the teachings of the Bible.

The last day that we were there, after all of the goodbyes to the students were said and tears were shed, we faced a few challenges. After swimming all week in the not-so-clean Adriatic, I wanted to do a little cleansing of everyone's ears using a method I had learned on the Amazon River: Pour a little peroxide in the canal and the little microbes that might have gotten in our ears were flushed out. It seemed to do the trick for everyone until I got to dear Jennifer. She had some issues with a hole in her ear drum, and my method caused her a great deal of pain.

Additionally, the guys were playing frisbee while waiting for our bus. Mike, the very amazing co-leader, was running to catch the frisbee when he fell into a huge aloe plant and sliced his cornea. When we arrived in Vienna, he spent most of his time in the hospital.

As we were walking through town, Jason, our wonderful detail-minded man on the team, was watching the men across the street play some games and walked into a lamppost. Immediately a HUGE egg-sized lump rose on his forehead. Ice is not something readily found in Kavaja, but I popped into a store and found a blue popsicle that did the trick, helping to reduce the swelling. (It also produced some interesting blue drips down his face and shirt.)

Another great lesson for a team leader: when you give people back home an itinerary and ask them to pray for the trip, have them start those prayers from the time you leave the U.S. and keep praying until the time you return. Things can happen.

The purpose of these short-term trips is two-fold: First, fulfill the requests of the partners serving in the different countries. Do a trip only if it fits their purposes and fulfills something that perhaps they can't do. In this case it was running an English camp. Second, plan so that the team members are mightily blessed by the experience.

There was such positive feedback when the team returned to church that, a few weeks later, the youth pastor asked if I would consider taking a team of teenagers to Kavaya the following year. Without a doubt I would do that! Mike agreed to go back as well. Rick, the youth pastor, would lead, and Mike and I would help. Mark and Keta were on board again. Sadly, a few months before we were to leave, Rick had a stroke and couldn't lead. Mike and I took the teens and led jointly.

The second camp had a much different feel. The size of the camp had doubled, and we had students from the ages of 10-25. One was in the army and a bouncer in a night club, and little Mohammed, whose parents wanted him to learn English, somehow squeezed in at 10!

Leading teams is like a progressive revelation; on each trip I learn at least one new thing. This time it was to label the luggage. We had packed up our suitcases with all of our supplies for teaching and crafts. We arrived at the airport with plenty of luggage, but it looked like some pieces were missing. The team assured me that the bags had all been in my dining room and I brought them all, so off we went. When we arrived in Albania and got settled at camp, we started looking for the supplies for our day-one activity. Nothing. Alas, we were missing two suitcases that had almost all of the crafts. That is when plan C (or maybe J) came into play. Sara and Robert, two teens from our church, were like "camp in a box." They were full of ideas and created a new plan without blinking an eye.

The Amazing Race was popular in the U.S. at the time, so they hastily planned a version of that: the GAR or Great Albanian Race. The 45 campers loved it! We watched the teams run off in all directions and hoped that they would all make it back. Two of our girls were gifted ballerinas, and one night they did an interpretive dance to "I Can Only Imagine." The girls danced with such feeling that it touched the hearts of everyone and words were not needed.

I could not have been more proud of that group of teens. Some were somewhat fussy at home about things they ate. On the trip, they ate everything served to them without a complaint. That might seem like a silly praise, but turning down food or being fussy would have been received as rudeness in that culture. The kids were gracious, polite and hardworking. They were creative and mostly flexible to the changes that came up along the way.

Some of the campers were grown men at 21-23 years old. That was somewhat intimidating as they were much bigger than our teens, and even bigger than Mike and I. God had the neatest plan for that. There was one young man who was particularly intimidating name Skard. Skard was strong, athletic, and not very friendly, but I think it was because he was shy. All week we could not break the ice with him. Mark, the resident worker there, did not care for the Adriatic Sea and was not overly excited about any of us swimming in it, particularly at night. One night we had all been playing volleyball before supper. It was hot, and we were all sweaty. Everyone ran to take a quick wash, but Skard got involved in something and didn't shower. After our meeting that night, one of the campers ran up to me and said that Mark was letting Skard swim in the sea. They wanted to go too. I was always up for an adventure, so I agreed. We got into our swim suits and, with lots of laughter, the 45 campers and the 14 team members went night swimming.

After about half an hour of playing in the water, I noticed some young men, not of our camp, who were quite inebriated. They were coming down the beach towards us. Just before I left North Carolina, Bob, a wise gentleman from our church, said to me, "Get the biggest and strongest guy on your side, and you will have an advocate forever."

Bobs' words came to mind, and I quickly found Skard not far from me in the water and told him I needed his help. I wanted him to help get all of our girls and campers out of the water immediately. Skard responded like a pro, and within minutes and without causing alarm, he became the leader, guiding and prodding, standing between us the uninvited inebriated ones. The remainder of the week, he was almost like a personal body guard and cheerleader for all that we had planned. Just a few choice words from a wise person like Bob, and God brings them to mind when they are needed.

How thankful I was for English Camp. I fulfilled the promise I had made to Mikel to go back and teach English to some of the young people. We made friends of the campers which gave our group a good reputation among the townspeople. And Mike and I really loved the group of teens who had come with us! They were young, but they were effective witnesses for God.

28

So Much Joy in Belarus

The Chernobyl disaster was a nuclear accident that occurred on 26 April 1986, in the country of Ukraine. It is considered the worst nuclear disaster in history, both in cost and casualties.

The long-term effects of the nuclear spill were felt for hundreds of miles, and one of the places where there was the most devastation was Belarus. Hundreds of young teens were diagnosed with thyroid cancer which affected their growth. Surgeries were often needed to correct cancer-related problems.

An SOS call came from Cary, a worker from GRE Mission whom we had met in Kosovo. It was a different kind of call. He asked if we could bring a team from our church to Sweden to work with Belarusian youth who had endured cancer surgeries. The plan was to get the teens away from their country and give them a place to breathe fresh, clean air, and a meaningful work project while they recovered. Lynn asked me to lead on this project, and I ended up working with the Belarusian group for two years.

Torchbearer International, a Bible school, was needing renovations on their buildings. It could be a good place for some of the teens to recuperate and get involved in a project. Twelve Belarusians would be selected and taken to Holsybrunn, a delightful, tiny Swedish town located half way between Copenhagen, Denmark and Stockholm, Sweden.

Our first church group was especially fun with three teens still in high school and three older folk who were in their seventies. Language barriers were overcome fairly easily, and when it was too hard, Irena or Mikhail, the Belarusian youth pastor and his wife, were be there to help. The young people from Belarus seemed excited to work. After trying to balance their thyroid levels for so long and feeling like invalids, they were free to be young; the work was hard and healthy.

Relationships were built and it was a precious time. The question from the campers on these trips was often: *What makes you different and why do you have so much joy?* The answer invariably is: We have the love of God and a relationship with Him.

Sweet Maria went to talk to Danielle from our church one evening and asked her how she could become a Christ follower. By the end of that conversation, Maria had chosen Christ. It was an encouragement to us all. Dema came from Belarus, sullen, angry, and for sure not interested in God or having a relationship with him. His life was rough back in Belarus, and his thyroid cancer added more stress. It was hard to penetrate his hardened heart. At camp, he tried new things and was surrounded by young people in the same boat as he, with the telltale scar across his neck. By the end of his time with all of the youth from his country and the team from America, you could see his heart softening. Our last night together, Dema decided that rather than fighting with a God who loved him, he wanted to get on the same side as God. The weeks we spent in Sweden were such a blessing.

***

Serving there in Sweden for two weeks each year for two years in a row allowed us to make friends. A few years later, it was a great honor when I was invited to come to Belarus to share at a reunion conference for the all the young people who had gone to Sweden. I had kept up with so many of them via email, but what a joy it would be to see them face to face again.

For this trip I had to leave on September 11–Lynn's birthday. He is and always has been my best friend and cheerleader. We had celebrated his birthday the night before and were having breakfast together as we turned on the TV. All the news was about the one-year anniversary of 9/11. It was such a solemn, sad reminder for this New York girl–the reminder of that tragedy was sobering and leaving my best friend at home was difficult. But following God's call was important.

The city of Minsk was much larger than I anticipated. It is the most populous city in Belarus and was teeming with young people. They held hands as they walked through the city parks, playing their music loudly. It was a vibrant city.

Mikhail, the Belarusian youth pastor with whom I had worked in Sweden, met me at the airport. We took the afternoon and drove to the work places of many of the ones who had been to Sweden. It was such a joy to see old friends. We went to the church where the meeting was about to start. I was joyful and tearful, getting to see these young people whom I had assumed I would never see again. Many of them were now strong in their faith and some were leaders at the church as well as working with the youth. A sweet girl named Yulia had been to camp. While there, she was not remotely interested in the things of God. After we greeted with big hugs, she openly admitted that she was very close to committing her life to God. She said, "Before, the most important thing to me was finances and my own happiness, but spiritual things are becoming more important to me now."

I had the privilege of speaking three times at the conference. No matter who was speaking, the young people were like sponges, wanting to soak up more about God. Between sessions the girls had so many questions. They constantly wanted to hold hands and be in contact. It was an amazing, touching time, literally and figuratively.

On Saturday night, after the teaching session, we all went out to celebrate the country's 93th anniversary of the founding of the BDR. We watched fireworks then girls persuaded me to dance to local folk music. I was probably awful, but the girls loved getting me to try new things. What a privilege to be part of their world of which they were so proud. Our bond became stronger.

Dima came to the whole conference. He told me that he was now active in a church in Brest, another large city. His smile still lit up the room. When he got to the camp in Sweden, he had been sullen and angry about the thyroid cancer. His life was dramatically changed while he was there. He surrendered his life to God and traded the anger for joy.

We traveled to villages in the area where so many of the students lived. As we walked into some of the villages, I kept gazing up on the roof tops looking for Tevye, from *"Fiddler on the Roof."* The houses looked like the movie; he could be singing and playing right there.

During the whole week in Minsk and the towns around it, I experienced surprise after surprise, seeing the transformation that God had brought about in so many young lives.

When first asked to lead a team to Sweden, I was reluctant. Beautiful, colorful Sweden? I was more used to serving in third-world countries. God's plan was totally different from my expectations. My heart was touched by all that God did as I realized again that God's plan is not bound by location. He challenges us to be ready to serve Him, anywhere, anyhow, and anytime. I am glad I answered His call.

29

Now You are Beautiful Yemen

Yemen is considered one of the oldest civilizations on earth, dating back to the area where Noah's son Shem settled. Another notable citizen of Yemen was reputed to be the Queen of Sheba. The country turned to Islam in the 7th century, and Yemen has been a tightly-held Muslim country since.

A couple from our church settled in Yemen. As Mission Pastors, Lynn and I visited them and it was such a privilege for us to experience life there prior to the country's closing to outsiders. We flew into the city of Sanaa and were picked up by friends. The antiquity of the city was evident. All women are required to wear a black Abaya and to cover every part of their body. One of our first stops was to the market to buy me a covering. An Abaya consists of a long black dress/coat that covers from the wrists to the toes. A black head covering completes the outfit.

I had chosen not to cover my complete face until we went into the old city. Vendors were selling their wares and there was a stall that sold the final piece–it left only the eyes exposed. We decided that maybe I should wear the entire outfit. An older man was the vendor of the face coverings. He took off my head piece, covered my face with his garment, and replaced the sheer black head dressing. He declared when my face and everything else was covered, "Now you are beautiful." I was not sure if that was a compliment or not, but I was complete and ready to spend the time appropriately in the country.

Even though every lady is covered head to toe in black, they seem to find a way to show their own fashion sense. There is bling on sleeves or on the hemline or on the scarves that cover their head. An inordinate amount of money is spent on mascara, since the eyes are the only thing shown to the public.

We were there over Valentine's Day. It is interesting that this holiday has traveled to all parts of the earth. On Valentine's Day, the department store windows are completely filled with long red strapless dresses, prom style, all varieties of red clothes, and very sexy negligees and underwear. This is not subtle: every store, everywhere displays roses and chocolates, huge red teddy bears, and long, poofy red dresses. How we longed to be able to share Jesus's love as obviously as they showed the red Valentine's Day love reminders in every single store.

***

We traveled to the second largest city in Yemen where our friends were working in a school teaching English. Taiz is nestled in a little valley, surrounded by hills. We were wakened early because each of the eight mosques around the house where we were staying started their worship at around 4 AM, but not all at the exact time. They each played a different tune or call, and at one point around 4:30, Lynn commented, "Now that's what you call a cacophony of calls to worship." The sounds echoed through the hills and went on for over an hour. Waking up early living there was a given.

We made another memory in the city. Lynn discovered after one dinner that he had lost a crown on a molar and the gaping hole made chewing quite uncomfortable. We still had two more weeks of travel and wanted to get it fixed somewhere.

We are all about new and fun experiences, and we found them in Taiz. The couple we were visiting were fairly new and had never been to a dentist, but through friends, we found one. He was amazing! He was originally trained in Moscow but had received a Master's degree in Iraq, a forensic dentistry degree in Germany, and had more degrees and certificates on his wall than we could have imagined! He spoke seven languages!! He was fascinating to meet and took Lynn in and worked on him immediately. The interesting thing is that here, the whole family comes in the exam room. The three of us were there saying our "oohs" and "awwws" at appropriate times as the doctor did injections and drillings and told us his whole life history while Lynn sat with his mouth open. The doctor was willing to do a whole new crown if we could stay another few weeks and it would cost about $100, but for the work that he did putting in a temporary crown, it cost $2.50. What a delightful experience! He could be working anywhere in the world, but has chosen to work in this rural city to help his people.

***

One night while we were in the city, we rode in the local van – a small bus of sorts that picks people up on the street. We went all the way to the top of one of the mountains surrounding the city. It cost ten cents to travel the entire route.

These vans were the mode of transportation that we used the entire time we were there because our friends did not own a car. Ladies, of course, sit with ladies because men are not allowed to sit next to a female. There is a constant shuffling of passengers when someone enters the van as they decided who could sit next to whom. The vans are old and rickety and sound like they are falling apart as they are spewing black smoke. There are hundreds of them on the streets. We had gone up to eat in a tiny little place that overlooks the city. We were able to pray for the people of the city and share some humus and beans. While we were there, three delightful completely-veiled young women came by to take photos of each other with the fantastic view in the background. I offered to take photos of the three of them together, using their camera, because they are not allowed to be photographed by others. My Arabic was not very good, but we had fun using hand signals and wound up talking for almost an hour. I have always longed, as I traveled, to be able to speak the heart language of every country and to be able to hear the stories of the people.

We jumped on a van to go back down the mountain, and this time there were 17 of us for the 12 seats available. We tried not to give a thought to whether or not the brakes were going to hold on our way down around the sharp curves. When we returned, we felt that after our 4 AM wake-up call and a very full day, that 9 PM would be a good time to say goodnight and get to bed. However, as we walked in the door, the phone was ringing. The neighbor thought this was a perfect time to teach me Arabic dancing. We went; we danced; we had refreshments; and we laughed until midnight. Another fun outing and cultural experience was the perfect ending to our time in Taiz.

We had heard our friends talk about *ghat*, but we did not really appreciate how much it had taken over the lives of the people there. At 1:00 PM, just about everything shuts down for the entire afternoon as people sit with a bag full of leaves, jamming them all in their mouth and chewing all afternoon. They don't swallow, but their side cheek gets huge and their teeth, green. It is NOT a pretty sight. They get an energetic buzz; it is the social activity of the day. They spend a lot of money buying the little plastic bags of it. Ladies chew; men chew; and teens chew. After the buzz comes the lethargy. This pastime almost controls the rhythm of the nation. One day, the plane that brings the ghat in didn't arrive. By evening and the next day, it seemed like the whole country was having withdrawal at the same time. Everyone was edgy and there was a tension in the air. It was the drug of choice for all the people in the whole country. We pray about the addiction when we pray for this land and its people.

***

The next day we went to the bus station to go back to the capital, Sanaa. Our host had taken our passports when we arrived, and he told us that he had to submit an application for us to be able to travel. After getting permission, our passports were returned. We had a long bus ride through mainly desert areas. At one point, our bus came to a stop in the middle of nowhere. Several armed men, each with an AK-47 rifle or a Kalashnikov automatic weapon, approached. It was a pretty imposing sight and a little startling as they boarded the bus, walked down the aisle, stopped at our seats, and asked for our papers. They didn't talk to anyone else. Despite being covered totally in black from head to toe and face, I guess my blue eyes were a giveaway. We were not seated near our hosts, therefore we could not understand what the soldier was saying, so we just followed the gestures of the man with the AK-47. Certainly, before we arrived there, we had heard of the kidnappings that were occurring in Yemen, so that thought concerned us. However, the man handed back our approved passes and left the bus. I wonder if he heard my sigh of relief when he departed the bus. The same thing happened two more times on our bus ride, but by the third time, it was not quite as much of a surprise.

When we arrived at our destination, we asked our friends what the stops were all about. They responded that those were the good guys, and they were there for our protection as foreigners, just confirming at the three check points that we were, in fact, still on the bus and safe. It would have been great to know that before we started, but it was nice to know that we were being cared for so nicely.

We admire the dear young couple we were visiting. Yemen is quite a challenging country in which to live, but they were obedient to what they believed God had called them to, and that was more important than their own personal comfort. A month after our visit, the director of the school where our friends were teaching was driving home from work when armed men pulled up beside him and shot and killed him. Our hearts ached for his family, as they counted the cost of serving. In spite of the fear, our friends loved the Yemeni people and enjoyed their jobs as English teachers. God gave them such a peace that they certainly didn't complain about their surrounding but had joy in the task before them. In the face of danger, inconveniences, depravation, and hardship, our friends keep their joy and continue to spread the love of our Lord to everyone they meet.

30

A Dry and Thirsty Land
Djibouti

When our time in Yemen was done, we flew over the Gulf of Aden, which is on the coast of North Africa, for our first visit to Djibouti, another Islamic country. Truth be told, I didn't have the slightest idea where this country was when we were setting our itinerary to visit another missionary couple from our church. (I'll call them J and K.)

The couple was posted in Somalia, but it was decided that since it is not safe for foreigners to have outside visitors there, we would meet them in Djibouti instead. We went because they were definitely in need of some encouragement. In Somalia there is an armed guard 24/7 posted outside the couple's door. If they need to go to the market for groceries, the guard hops on the back of the motorbike and goes to shop with J. When J plays soccer, the armed guard is with him at all times. It was decided that J and K could enjoy a pastoral visit much more if they were free to interact without their armed guard around, thus they arranged for all of us to stay at another friend's home in Djibouti. The privilege of seeing the workers in this "dry and thirsty land" has been one that will remain in our hearts forever, recognizing the challenges for partners working in this part of the world.

One of the blessings for us personally was that we rarely experienced jet lag when we traveled. The flights to the Middle East and North Africa, especially, come and go between midnight and 4 AM. The flights are long, and if we are staying with a family only four days, we want to be sharp and ready to go as soon as we get off the plane. We did not want to waste a minute of our time together being sleepy.

Djibouti is a desert country. It is reported that they get rain only four or five days for the entire year. Interestingly, it rained the night that we arrived, and for two of the four days, heavy rains that soaked everything. In a town with no sidewalks, the whole town becomes a running stream with mud and sewage running through it. Many of the people live in tiny tin houses which leak.

When we were in Yemen, I dressed totally in black, as did every woman on the street. When we arrived in Djibouti, we found that fashion is just the opposite. It is an Islamic country, but the black attire was replaced with bright, flowing dresses. The everyday dress is much like a Hawaiian muu-muu except they are long, down to the floor, and are called a "sheet." They are huge and very flowing and cool. An elaborate petticoat is worn underneath; it also goes to the floor and has a foot of lace along the bottom edge. It is fashionable to lift the upper skirt when walking through the streets to avoid the dirt and mud, but acceptable to allow the lacey petticoat to show. A large shawl is worn over the shoulders and covering the head. In Yemen, the face could not be exposed, but in Djibouti, the entire face can show. It has been interesting to note the similarities and the differences in two Islamic countries that are separated by a small strait of water.

Our hosts here were so gracious. They, like the friends in Yemen, have chosen to live a very simple lifestyle, similar to the people with whom they work. The house is basic but adequate and certainly not ostentatious. The small bathroom is a simple room with a toilet that is flushed from a bucket; water is kept in a large barrel nearby. The shower head is in the middle of the room and runs only a small trickle of cold water. There is no mirror or sink or cupboards. Rubber sandals are worn because no matter what one goes in the bathroom for, the feet get pretty wet. We did not have a mirror the whole time we were in the two countries and that has its advantages! Lynn put his contacts in from his reflection in a photo frame on their dresser. We had electricity, so I could blow dry my hair but had NO IDEA what it looked like. We wore a head scarf every time we went out, coming back sweaty and dripping from the high temperatures or the rain. It was probably a good thing we could not see what we looked like.

Our host family's home had electricity most of the time, with a generous sprinkling of power cuts, but of course, there was no internet, nor was there any in the town. To send email, they would have to travel to the city by bus, about a half-hour ride away, and they paid to use an internet cafe. There was no TV or radio, so we all had no idea what was happening in the rest of the world. That was okay. We were 100% there!

Our hosts lived on the roof which is the third floor. Their apartment has no outside walls, but there are inside partitions and a covering over most of the home. Their sitting room is open, but because there is a constant breeze, it is comfortable. The days in the summer months average 130 degrees in that part of the desert. Parts of their home have cement lattice work which provides a wonderful breeze day and night. However, there are lots of mosquitoes that carry Dengue fever. Their apartment is on the main road, so there is an amazing cacophony of sounds all day long: trucks, buses, cars, goats, children, venders passing by, and someone else's music. The call to prayer five times a day is a constant, as it is in Yemen. Of course, the sound comes from the many surrounding mosques and as in Yemen, the mosque calls are not syncopated, so they come often and the sounds are from many directions, similar what we heard in Taiz.

Since the country is a French colony, the "baguette" is the bread of choice; we bought one each morning for around ten cents. Our hostess took us for an hour's walk to the market for bread, going up and down the hills. When we started out that morning, she reminded us that MOST of the Djiboutians are a wonderful, friendly people. But some are not thrilled that there are "infidels" (non-Muslims) living in their town. She said, "Please don't take it as an affront if rocks are thrown at us. It is not the typical attitude of most of the people, but it does happen."

***

One of the more strange or interesting experiences was the night we wanted to take the two couples out for dinner. We needed to change our U.S. money to Djiboutian francs to pay for dinner. There were no banks, so money is changed on the black market. The money changes were made almost exclusively by older ladies sitting on the curbs along the streets. Since it had been raining, the transaction places were muddy. It wasn't an easy process. The "would be bankers" would take only $20 bills. Each bill was examined with great care. If there was the tiniest wrinkle or writing or spots, these ladies would not exchange them.

We finally managed to get a sufficient amount of money exchanged and proceeded to drive into the city to run a few errands, confirm our return flights, and have a fun dinner. As we drove to town, we passed a herd of about 200 camels that were in a holding pen waiting to be shipped to Egypt. It was a fascinating sight to see. We were used to seeing one lone camel feeding on a tree, so seeing that herd was a particular delight.

One of the things that was overwhelmingly obvious about both of the couples that we visited is the love that they have for the people that God had called them to live and work with. Both of their environments were hard, and yet the people won their hearts. Both couples have attitudes that reflect that which is written in Philippians 2: they have servant hearts; they give of themselves without reserve. The many things that could be taken as inconveniences, they are counting as privileges. They both, serving in two challenging countries and with all of the difficulties of their living conditions, are excited to serve. Their prayer was to have the opportunity to tell their neighbors about God's love, and it is happening. What a privilege to see them first-hand doing what they came to do.

***

One morning, as I sat doing some writing, there was a knock on our third-floor door. As J opened the door, there was a young man, perhaps about 30 years old, who was crippled. He had climbed up the stairs using only his arms and dragging his legs behind him. J had told him that he had found a wheelchair for him, and the young man wanted to see it. I was sitting in the corner of the veranda, and I wished so much that it would not have been rude for me to video what was going on. J was sitting next to him on the floor. J told me later that he didn't want to appear to be looking down on his guest, so they just sat talking. The guest was mentioning that he will have to strengthen his arms to be able to wheel his new chair along the rutted and dusty roads of Djibouti. J showed him some weights that he had made. They were two bleach bottles with the tops cut off, and J filled them with cement and put a bar between the two to make dumbbell. J had made several sizes, from vegetable tins to paint cans, all filled with cement, as a gift for the young man. He wants to be able to play wheelchair basketball with some guys in the neighborhood.

As we watched these two young couples in Yemen and Djibouti, we were blessed to see friendship evangelism at work. The attitude of both of the couples was amazing! They lived with so little if it were measured in human comforts, but I don't think they even realized that. We never heard one complaint or picked up a hint of resentment for the things that they left behind. It is refreshing to observe this attitude. Both couples keep reminding us what a privilege it is to serve the people around them. They know that it is hard, dry ground that they have been given in which to work, and what they readily do is "count it all JOY."

They are HUMBLING....AMAZING......and INSPIRING!

As always, Lynn and I feel that we were the ones who were BLESSED just to come alongside the partners and watch God at work. We went to be the encouragers, and we left being the blessed ones.

31

Three Amazing People
Zimbabwe

Westover Church, in Greensboro, North Carolina, had been a missions-minded church for both local and global outreach for 50 years when Lynn was hired as the first Global Pastor. His job description for this new position was very basic and in three areas: Be a pastor to our missionaries; develop a focus for our outreach program; and educate and motivate the church family to the opportunities to serve.

Many months were spent developing the outreach focus: A ten-year vision and plan to focus on the Muslim and Hindu worlds and the people of China. It would not take away from the partners that we already worked with, but would give us more awareness of those areas.

Lynn grew up in Africa and the two of us served together in Zimbabwe, so it would have been easy for us to look only at the needs of the HIV/AIDS pandemic that was devastating the continent. However, we never wanted to show favoritism to the country that we held so dear to our hearts.

The entire pastoral staff went to a conference held by a large church in Illinois. One of the speakers was a singer named Bono, who was very involved in the AIDS pandemic. One of the statements he made was that every church in the USA should be involved somehow in helping the people in Africa with the widespread AIDS problem. When the staff returned to the church, they asked Lynn at their next meeting: "Why is our church not involved in this great need?" Lynn was ready to jump on board and get involved, with the blessing of the pastors.

A vision team of four men made a trip to Zimbabwe shortly after that. God opened door after door through the contacts that we already had in the country. Lynn asked the same question of each of the leaders he met that he asked before we entered the China focus: Is there a way that our church could be involved without disrupting what you are already doing? The answer was a resounding YES, and so began the new partnership to help in Zimbabwe.

Sadly, HIV/AIDS was going through the continent like wild fire. It was tragic. Food was needed; medicines were needed; and the number of orphans in Zimbabwe alone was about two million. How does one even begin to help? Churches were motivated to get involved and began setting up stations where families would come and get food at least. Many children were alone, living in homes with elderly grandparents because they had lost one or both parents.

The Shona people are very familial. Typical orphanages were not the best solution. A group came in and started setting up homes with 12-14 orphans, an Aunty, and two helpers for cooking and laundry. The children were settled into a more home-like situation with their own rooms and clothes and places to study.

Lucy's Story

Lucy lost both her parents within six months when she was ten years-old. She was blessed by being able to live in one of the homes that was set up for orphans. Lucy was quite shy and never felt comfortable with new people but had a huge smile that belied the emptiness that she felt in her heart. When she was a teenager, a new couple came into her life: Garikai and Virginia. A special bond was built between them, and they started spending weekends together. Often Lucy was introduced as their first-born child and, for the first time since her parents passed, she began to feel secure and loved. Lucy remembers feeling like she belonged, and her smile was now genuine.

We first met Lucy when she had just come to the home. She had a beautiful voice and sang often when we visited. Years later we were coming back to start doing camps with the children from the homes. We called those camps, Camp Allelu, and we met out at a beautiful piece of property that had enough little huts to house about 50 children at a time. Through the years of that focus, well over 130 people from our church went to serve the children there and special bonds were forged. But a highlight for our visits was Lucy. She came now as an older teen and worked at the camp, cooking and doing whatever needed to be done to make those children feel at home.

At one of our camps, Lucy expressed her joy of sewing. Virginia was a gifted seamstress, and God had put on her heart the desire to start a sewing school so that when these girls aged out of the homes, they would have a marketable skill. That was a concern that we had with the government orphanages: when the children were 18 years of age, they were considered aged-out. They were required to leave the orphanage and find work. Sadly, if they had no skills, both boys and girls would land on the streets, and their futures were uncertain.

Virginia's desire for a school and Lucy's desire to sew fit together. The first team that I had the privilege of leading there had their hearts touched by sweet Lucy's testimony. We bought her a sewing machine to get her started. Lucy and Virginia continue this passion, and hundreds of girls now leave the homes with a sewing skill.

Lucy credits the nurturing of Garikai and Virginia in the preparation for her life. "They saw something in me before I ever did and helped me become the woman that I am today," says Lucy. She has gone on to Bible School and met a wonderful man named Lovemore at church. They readily received the blessing of Garikai and Virginia, and they are pastoring and leading a

Lovemore, Lucy and their children

church in Harare. Being a pastor's wife in Zimbabwe means she is automatically the leader of the women's department. It has been a wonderful opportunity for Lucy to teach women to sew and sell their items which brings in money for their childrens' school fees. Together Lucy and Lovemore have invested in the youth of their church, and a new generation is being raised up following Jesus.

Garikai and Virginia's Story

We met Garikai in 2006 when we started connecting with the Hand of Hope feeding program. He had started his burden for the many orphans in Zimbabwe in 2001. Garikai had a heart to learn more about God's word and started meeting with Pastor Matatu. However, the pastor's priority was to live out the Scriptures by "feeding the orphans." He was trying to get Garikai interested in working in the orphan community. Pastor Matatu had a tiny piece of land by the parsonage where he grew vegetables and used them to feed scores of children every day at noon. Garikai remembered that when he was growing up, he watched a grandmother care for her three young grandchildren after her son and daughter-in-law had died of HIV, and his heart was broken. It was a natural transition for him to step into a ministry that had a heart for orphans. He joined with Hands of Hope Ministry and became an integral part of it. Even though they were working with hundreds of orphans, Garikai seemed to know every child and each of their stories, and he became a substitute dad for many.

Virginia and Garikai met and were married in 2007. Garikai was teaching and Virginia also wanted to teach. Their plan was to work together as a family. Their vision changed the more time they spent with the orphans. Their passion was for the aged-out boys and girls who had nothing to do. Virginia entered university with the goal of starting a sewing-skills school so the girls would have a skill to support themselves. Through the years, God has blessed the program and several of the girls are now sewing for reputable companies in Harare to support themselves.

Garikai and Virginia

Hearing Garikai's and Virginia's story and the passion they have for orphans impacted my heart so much. I brought a team from our church to hold a camp doing crafts, teaching soccer, and sharing stories of God's love. One night, Garikai shared a deeply painful experience with the team. I want to share that, with his permission, in his words.

"My dear Virginia lost our first baby at full term. We arrived at the hospital when she was in labor. The entire medical staff, both nurses and doctors, were on strike. We were left in the waiting room; complications occurred and as a result, we lost our child. Children are a blessing from the Lord, and this was incredibly painful. Our second pregnancy came as a much-needed solace to both of us, but this pregnancy ended in a miscarriage at fourmonths. Our pain was so intense. In our culture having a child is extremely important. Our ministry together was with orphans, and I remember putting on a brave face and ignoring our private pains.

That same year Judy and the team from Westover came to work with the orphans. Judy identified our pain and started casual therapeutic counseling with us, and she ensured us that God was still for us. I think living in the Shona culture, she knew the value in our culture of having children soon after marriage. Both Virginia and I have been Christians from our youth, yet we were not spared the fears that came which were influenced by our cultural beliefs. I remember how our ministry to orphans was being affected by our own private grief. There were memories of our two lost sons, always lingering in the back of our minds as we were ministering to hurting children. Judy could have stopped after giving Virginia and me grief counseling, but she did not.

She felt that we needed time alone, away from the daily demands of our work. The last night that we were together with the team, Judy and her team had a time of communion and foot washing for those of us on staff. I remember the team laying hands and praying over Virginia and me as they asked God to bless us with a child, if it were His will. Then they sent us off with a gift of a three-day stay at a safari lodge. We remember the three days for more than the scenic views and hospitality we received. Exactly nine months after that holiday, God gave us a son. Later that year we were brought to North Carolina to be part of the Global Conference. One of my friends saw the photos of my time there that I had posted on Facebook. I will never forget his comment: 'from zero to hero.' Some would find this trite statement needlessly insensitive. Truth be told, there was no better statement which could sum up my story that those words. God sent a team to bring healing to our hearts."

Three people I remember vividly from Zimbabwe: Lucy, Virginia, and Garikai. Although we no longer serve in that country, we so often think about these three amazing people, serving God faithfully with all their hearts, and we see the precious fruit of their labor.

32

Dorothy and The Goats
Zimbabwe

The Karanda Mission Hospital, in the northeast quadrant of Zimbabwe, has been an oasis for more people than one could count. The dedicated doctors and nurses have had a special calling to be able to accomplish all they have done, tirelessly and all to honor God.

During the years of the war of independence in the 1970's and 1980's, they treated many patients from landmine victims and people who had been terrorized and maimed, to the normal everyday births and operations. During the time of the HIV pandemic, special orphan days were held once a month. Children would walk up to ten kilometers to attend and they would play games and get good food and other treats. There were many "orphan-led villages" where children who had lost both parents to HIV were being brought up by the oldest child in the family. When I had an accident with boiling water in language school, KMH was the place I went to be treated.

When my dad was a young child, he burned his hand on a steam pipe. As he aged, his whole hand closed up, making it very difficult to hold the steering wheel on his tugboat. He tried so many places to have it cared for in the USA, but doctors were reluctant to do it. My dad was frustrated. I asked him to wait until he came to Zimbabwe; I knew that Doctor Stephens would fix it. Roland Stephens never said No to a challenge. When the freedom fighters would come in to a village to terrorize the people, often they would cut off ears or lips. People were maimed and scarred. Doctor Stephens was known to "make new lips or ears" and repair them.

Karanda had and still has, one of the best nurse's training and midwife training programs in the whole country. When we were living in Africa, the outpatient areas were filled with ox carts bringing in patients. In recent years, the parking lot is filled with cars from all over the country. People will bypass the hospitals in the capital city and drive hours to get to rural Karanda because of the excellent care they know they will receive.

During our time at Kapfundi, one of the highlights of the month was when a doctor and nurse from Karanda Hospital would fly in the little Cessna and spend the day treating the more difficult cases of our small clinic. Lynn's mom and dad were living in Karanda at the time. Dad was the chaplain and Mom was in charge of the Tuberculosis ward. It is part of the Shona culture that when the grandmother requests to have a grandchild visit, one is expected to comply. After a visit by the medical team, Grandma asked if our daughter Kim could visit her for a bit. We packed her little suitcase, including her white apron with a red cross on front and her nurse's hat, and sent our little blonde four-year-old off on the Cessna to spend time with her grandparents. (I shed some tears, but what an experience for Kim and Grandma to work together in the hospital!)

The hospital hours were long and often very hard for the medical staff. They were tired and sometimes discouraged by the case load they carried, especially during the days of the HIV/AIDS pandemic. One of the doctors said to us, "I trained for years to heal and help people. With this HIV pandemic, I sustain the life of someone with AIDS, but I am mainly preparing them for death." Thankfully new drugs were discovered, and they made significant changes in the lives of people.

Lynn's mom told us that one day at their staff gathering, when so many were exhausted and discouraged, someone taught them this song:

> *"It's amazing what praising can do*
> *It's amazing what praising can do*
> *I don't worry when things go wrong*
> *Jesus fills my heart with a song"*

So many things are about *our* focus. When everything around looks gray and discouraging, if we realign our focus towards Jesus, it impacts our lives.

***

A dear saint who impacted my life is Dorothy, a nurse who worked in the Nursing School at Karanda. She was born into a broken home. Her dad was an alcoholic, and they lived in the southern part of Zimbabwe. The country had two main tribes, Shona in the North and Ndebele in the South; the two languages and cultures were quite different.

Dorothy, a dear saint

When Dorothy was a young teen, she was invited to live with a missionary family in Bulawayo, a city in the south of Zimbabwe. She was raised by the Byrmo family, who took in other young girls as well. The Byrmos invested in those girls at a crucial time in their young lives. Dorothy's mom was a nurse and

Dorothy wanted to follow in her mother's footsteps. Through the Byrmo family, she heard about the nursing school at Karanda, and she traveled to start her training. When she graduated from nurse's training, she returned to Bulawayo, worked there, and met her husband, Obvious Chirindo. The situation in Karanda became quite dangerous, and there were several frightening and upsetting visits from the freedom fighters. It was decided that the hospital would close for a while.

When the hospital reopened some years later, Dorothy and her husband were asked to go back to Karanda. She started working at the hospital, but being a gifted nurse with wonderful teaching skills, she was soon invited to join the staff at the nursing school.

During that time, Dorothy decided to get her bachelor's degree in the town of Bindura. Her area of research was something that was deeply on her heart during this time of the HIV pandemic. Sick moms with AIDS usually could produce no milk for their babies. Her project for her degree: persuade the Shona moms to be receptive to using goat's milk for their babies. Goats were everywhere, but goat's milk was not usually used for humans. After much research, it was determined that the moms would be willing to try.

It was about that time, in June, 2006, that Lynn was visiting Karanda on a trip from the USA. He was walking through the wards at the hospital with Dorothy. They stopped at the bed of a young mother and her tiny baby who was crying. The baby's grandma was standing next to the bed and Lynn and Dorothy stopped to talk to them. The grandmother, looked at Lynn and explained, almost apologetically, about her grandson's crying. "My daughter has HIV/AIDS and the baby was also born with it. She has no milk to nurse him, and the emaciated baby cries all the time. We can't afford to buy formula from the stores, so now our hearts hurt and we all cry."

Lynn was moved with compassion. Dorothy, who was in the middle of her research for her degree, shared her idea with Lynn. "If we could get a nursing goat and give it to each mom who can't produce milk, it would be a solution for these families and give the baby a chance in life."

Dorothy knew that this would work. In 2004, she had found a baby in the bushes by the hospital. Some mom who perhaps had little hope for this child had left him. When Dorothy found him, he was brand new but already grossly underweight. He did not tolerate formula of any type. No one came to claim the baby, and Dorothy decided to care for him herself. She had tried cow's milk, but he could not tolerate that; so when Dorothy found a little nursing goat she tried that and the baby tolerated the goat milk well.

Dorothy told Lynn as they stood in the hospital, "As my love for this little boy, whom I named Innocent, grew, my love for goat's milk grew as well. Innocent started growing and gaining weight. I knew that this would work for other babies who could not breast feed. If I could find goats for them, it would keep them from dying from malnutrition."

Lynn asked Dorothy how much a nursing goat costs. She said that one could be bought in a village for about $15.

This was a huge takeaway for Lynn while he was on that first survey trip. He came back to the USA and shared this story with our church. He did not share it to be a fundraiser, but he wanted people to hear both the story of Innocent, who was thriving, and this little infant he met at the hospital.

At the end of the service, very much to his surprise, a stream of people came to find him. "Here is $15. Can I buy a goat for Dorothy's dream?"

Over and over through the weeks that followed, the project grew. Some fathers pulled out a picture of a goat from their wallets. "Guess what my kids gave me for Fathers' Day? Two goats!"

Dorothy's vision that God put on her heart kept multiplying. We kept sending funds, and she kept buying goats. So many goats were bought that we soon sent money for a goat pen and little houses for the goats, and then some more for a goat herder. What a joy to send our senior pastor back four years later to see dozens of goats and their nursing human babies. The lives of babies were saved because an amazing woman found a discarded baby in a bush and had an idea of how to help. Her life had been rescued and given meaning by a missionary family, and she was doing the same for Innocent and hundreds of other babies.

The care-givers of Karanda Hospital were phenomenal. Their work blessed the people in the surrounding area and was testimony to the love of God. They lived out the command from James, *"Be ye doers of the word and not hearers only."*

33

Faith Stories from
Lebanon and Jordan

As we were wrapping up our three-and-a-half-year focus on the Muslim world in 2009, we traveled to another part of the Middle East. Meeting the believers there was such an encouragement to our hearts. We had the privilege of hearing the stories of the Christ followers and all that they have been through.

Our trip took us first to Beirut, Lebanon. Vern, an Elder of our church, accompanied us. The Bible talks about a city on the hill that cannot be hidfrn, and that was what first impacted me as we flew into Beirut at 3:30 AM. We had been told that we would easily recognize the twinkling lights of the Bible college that we were visiting. The college, which was sitting on the top of one of the hills was easily visible as we landed. We were taken to the school and caught a few hours' sleep and then had the rest of the day to talk with some of the students from the college. After talking to just five or six of the students enrolled from all over the middle east, we found that the school was truly a beacon for God in that city.

In the 1980's, this small country, only 200 miles long and very narrow, saw the deaths of more than 100,000 people. Again in 2008, another civil war broke out and thousands more were killed. What a transformation in such a small county, where almost every family lost at least one member! During our time there, we had the privilege of meeting with both people who lived there all their lives and refugees who had fled there.

***

We sat one morning with a dear 80-year-old woman named Njila. Her name means "shining, brilliant and glistening," and I believe her parents named her well. We talked with her over breakfast and her gorgeous smile lit up the room. She and her husband had raised three sons. During the 1980's war, they had lost their home and the family of five had to start life completely over again. What a joy to hear that all of her sons are following God, that bitterness was not part of their lives. Scripture talks about loving your neighbor, and yet her home was destroyed completely by her neighbors. I asked her how she managed to raise three boys in the midst of the killing and bombings and losing everything they owned. These sons are men of faith who have vibrant ministries for God along with great attitudes.

Her reply came readily. "My husband and I needed to teach our children to love God no matter what their circumstances. As parents we worked hard to help them pull out any roots of bitterness that might have grown in them."

One of her sons was sitting with us and said, "We were raised very poor but never realized it because there was so much joy in our home."

So many of the believers that we met in that war-torn country were obviously walking close to God, and the lessons that they learned during those horrific times blessed and encouraged me.

***

Back at the Bible college, we heard the story of Mohammed, a young Muslim man who grew up in Sudan. While living in a small village in North Africa, he had heard about the man Jesus from a couple passing through their area. Mohammed was intrigued by the stories they shared, and he wanted to learn more about this prophet. Proselytizing and conversion to a different faith were illegal in an Islamic village, but the more he studied and learned, the more he knew he wanted to become a Christ follower. He was so impacted by Christ that he shared his decision with the leaders in his village, knowing the cost that he might pay. The leaders did not accept his decision to follow the one they called Infidel. Mohammed was placed on a chair in the middle of their village and was told that he had to denounce his faith and his conversion. He refused. He was given other opportunities to recant, but he still refused. Villagers then proceeded to bully him and beat him to try to get him to change his mind, and he refused to denounce his faith in Christ. Mohammed was then stabbed repeatedly by men of the village, and still refusing to submit, he finally died.

Mohammed's younger brother, Ibrahim, stood back watching as the life ebbed out of his older brother. He could not believe Mohammed's strong faith, and it emboldened Ibrahim to study the Bible on his own and learn more about Jesus's teachings. We had the privilege to meet and have lunch with Ibrahim and hear this story as well as his own personal journey in becoming a Christ follower. A group from the Bible college was visiting his village in North Africa and invited him to come to Beirut to study at the Bible college. Knowing what the cost could be, still his desire was to become a pastor, return to Sudan and share the truths he had found in the Bible.

We left Lebanon encouraged, recognizing how easy it was for us as North Americans to live out our faith in a country with freedom of religion. The examples of faith that we met along our way were many.

***

Jordan was next on our itinerary and our time there was equally encouraging. Jordan is an ancient country but there was an amazing combination of old and new. The city of Amman was modern and yet in other areas of Jordan, the Roman chariot wheels that had chiseled ruts in the cobble-stoned streets were still visible. Jordan is flooded with refugees from the surrounding countries of Iraq and Palestine. Because of the repeated wars and political disruptions, people have been driven from their home countries. The refugees are finding in Jordan a freedom to seek a relationship with God that they were not allowed to have in their home country. The church in Jordan was growing rapidly, and the testimonies that we heard were compelling.

Anna, a beautiful Iraqi woman, was another jewel whom we had the privilege of meeting. Her dad was the governor of Basra, Iraq. He was killed, along with her brother in a conflict in Iraq. Several months later, her mom died of what the doctor believed was a broken heart shortly after losing her husband and son. Anna was married at 16 and got pregnant shortly after. Her husband was in the Iraqi army and was one of the body guards for Saddam Hussein. He was killed during his service. At 23, Ashley was both an orphan and a widow with two young children. She had no brother or family to care for her. She fled from Iraq and went to Jordan where she found a new faith in Jesus and developed a vibrant relationship with God. When we met her, we were reminded about what we read about the Apostle Paul. Her desire was to share Jesus with anyone she met. Just meeting her and hearing her story was such an encouragement.

Walking where Jesus walked in the country of Jordan was very special. Seeing first-hand that He is alive and working in the hearts of people, just as He did when He lived in the Middle East, was the most amazing and thrilling part of our trip.

34

They Call Her Blessed Zimbabwe

Throughout our years of traveling, there are many people who have truly impacted my life. I would like to share about one in particular, whose life has been a beacon to me: "Gogo" Editor Mawire, from Zimbabwe.

Throughout our travels to Zimbabwe, Africa, our lives have intersected on several occasions with Mrs. Mawire. When we moved to Kapfundi in 1969, Mrs. Mawire and her husband were already living there. Mr. Mawire was teaching at the school that was located on our mission station. He and his wife and children were all involved in the local church. They had a teacher's house on the station, but their village was also located not far from our mission station across the Badzi River.

In most all village settings, even to this day, there is no electricity. The water for the cooking and bathing and watering their garden is available when someone from the family walks to the river with a clay pot, fills the pot, and walks home. The clay pots were brought back to their villages, usually carried beautifully poised on the heads of the moms or young girls. I would see them walking with a pot of water on their head, usually with a baby sitting on their back, held tight with a towel around the size of a beach towel. Often, to my amazement, since their hands were empty, they were knitting as they walked along.

Cooking for their family was accomplished on a small fire in the middle of the cooking hut, not on a bottled-gas stove. To make that fire, someone, usually a child, had to chop wood or collect fallen branches to provide the wood.

Often the children had to do these chores before walking miles to school. Uniforms were required at school and books had to be purchased. In a pretty much non-cash society, purchasing those items was a challenge. The fathers often went many miles away to the capital city to work, only coming home to the village on their annual vacation.

Rural women in Zimbabwe work very hard, and they are to be admired as they handle so many tasks. Proverbs 31 talks about a very special woman, who seemed to be able to accomplish more than one could conceive. She worked at home, raised her children, cooked, sewed, and so much more, often in adverse conditions.

I better understood that passage from the Bible when I moved to Kapfundi. Gogo (which means Grandmother in Ndebele) Mawire is one of the dear Saints who had a significant impact on my life. As of this writing she is almost 80 years old.

Editor was married to Solomon Mawire for 42 years. Solomon was an educated man, and had a variety of jobs and training before we met him at Kapfundi Mission, where he was eventually promoted to headmaster of our local school. Editor was a housewife in a very rural area, so for much of her life, she performed the duties that I listed above. Most of her married years she spent working their home farm plots during planting and harvesting times. On rural land, with no electricity, no running water, no indoor plumbing was how she was used to living. Her sweet husband Solomon passed away in 2002, and Editor has been running the farm since then. In the year 2017, she harvested 11 tons of maize, one ton of soy beans, 26 bales of sunflowers, as well as paprika and ground nuts.

Judy with the joyful Gogo Maywire

Gogo Mawire has five children, eleven grandchildren, and six great-grandchildren. Because of their hard work, all of her children managed to go to boarding school and excelled in their studies. Education was a priority for their family. Editor was very involved in the Kapfundi Evangelical Church. The example that she and her husband set for the children was ingrained in each of them. Now each of their children is also involved in serving God. Judith, the oldest, is the district chairperson for the evangelical church. Gogo's second born, Dr. Collett Mawire, is a gynecologist. He has been the Provincial Medical Superintendent of a large hospital in Zimbabwe where his wife also works. Gallington is their third child. He majored in finance and works as Deputy Director of Zimbabwe's reserve bank. Gallington is married with two boys and also serves as an associate pastor in Harare, the capital city. Gogo Mawire's fourth son, Wellington, is a financial consultant as well as being very involved at his church. Ronald is the youngest and is involved in teaching and is on their church board.

When one speaks with the five children of Gogo Mawire, they echo the words of Proverbs 31: "They rise up and call her

Blessed." Imagine her life: living in a rural place with no wash-er, dryer or what we would consider modern conveniences. Yet she has incredible joy and has raised such successful children who not only have achieved status in the world, but each of them is also a Christ follower and leader in their church. She has been an example of a hard-working, God-fearing woman and an inspiration and role model to me. I thank God for the privilege of knowing her.

35

A Precious Family Treasure
and A Map of Memories

Back in the 1950's Lynn's dad built the house that their family of six lived in at Kapfundi Mission. It was made of ant hill dirt with a metal roof. When Dad built the fireplace, it was made of brick, with an overlay of pieces of slate. One of the pieces of slate looked very much like the map of the continent of Africa. It was customary for Lynn and his siblings to sit on the hearth of that fireplace and have family tea. It is also one of my beloved husband's favorite memories of living in that house.

When we arrived at Kapfundi in 1969, our first assignment after language school was to move into that same house. Kim was an only child at that point and then Rick came along in 1971. What a joy it was for our children to sit at the very same fireplace, having their tea, where their dad and uncles and aunt had sat so many years earlier.

Years later, Lynn was asked to speak at a celebration conference in Zimbabwe. After the conference, we made the long trip out to Kapfundi. We had not visited there since we left in 1976. Our house was no longer standing, and the only thing left was the fireplace. We walked around the footprint of the house, remembering each of the rooms and then stood in front of that fireplace that held such happy memories for the two Everswick

families that had lived there. When I saw that the slate map of Africa was still there and completely intact, I had an idea. I wrote to the Bishop of the Evangelical Church and asked, since the house was no longer standing, if there would be any chance of my removing that piece the next time I visited Africa. I thought it would be a wonderful gift to present to Lynn for his 70th birthday as a reminder of the two times he had lived there in that home. The bishop agreed.

A few years later I was in Zimbabwe with a short-term team. My dear friend Pat offered to drive out to Kapfundi in their truck. I asked Jeff, one of our team members who was so handy, if he would drive out with us and see if that one piece of slate could be removed from the fireplace.

We arrived on a Friday afternoon in 2016. The very next morning, ignoring jetlag, we made what was about a five-hour drive out to Kapfundi. A precious friend, Philip Hwamaridza, who used to live in that area, went with us to the old site, as there are no road signs to get there. (Directions were turn right at that big baobab tree. Go left at that water pump.) We made it safely and we found our beloved house. The fireplace was still standing. We took quite a few photos, because we were not sure if the slate would hold up as the men tried to extricate it. After all, it had been sitting in that place for almost 60 years.

It took almost no time for Jeff to get it off. Such joy at thinking what a surprise it would be for Lynn to hang in his office. We had been making preparations for the Global Conference to be held at our church that fall. Because it is one of Lynn's favorite reminders (and his dad's as well), it was decided that the theme of the conference would be, "Do you know that Jesus loves you?" The short-term team that was serving with me at Camp Allelu in Zimbabwe convinced me that rather than give the slate to Lynn for his September, birthday, we should save it for the November missions conference. And we did.

I wrote to our global partners around the world and asked each if they could video their family saying the phrase, "Do you know Jesus loves you?" in the language of the country where they were serving. The video clip was put together, and it was so fun. Lynn had no idea what we were doing until Sunday morning of the conference. We showed the video of Global workers, as well as our five children, greeting us. Then Lynn was presented with the piece of slate in the shape of Africa, framed beautifully by Jeff with the words: "Do you know Jesus Loves you?"

Now that framed piece of memorabilia hangs over our fireplace in Texas and the third generation of grandchildren sit and enjoy their tea under the map. We feel so honored by the heritage with which God has blessed us.

36

Rathana's Testimony
Cambodia

The Lord is a refuge for the oppressed,
a stronghold in times of trouble. Psalms 9:9

These words from Psalm 9 would not have come easily to the mind of Rathana, a young man from Cambodia who suffered much, in his early life. It wasn't until much later that he realized God had His hand on him and would use the challenges he faced to become foundational steps in his life.

In 2011, Lynn and I had the very special privilege of making our first visit to Cambodia. I did not realize at the time that it would be the first of eight consecutive years of spending the whole month of January living in a dorm in Phnom Penh; years that hold such fond memories of such beautiful people.

Our plan for that first visit was to go to Singapore on behalf of our church to visit an amazing Chinese man named Paul. The church had supported Paul financially and in prayer for more than 40 years, and this was the first official visit that our church had made to him. Paul was living and serving in Singapore, but the focus of his organization was working in several Southeast Asian countries. Paul asked if, instead of spending our time with him in Singapore, we would be willing to accompany him and travel to one of his ministry areas in the country of Cambodia.

I must admit, we did not know much about the country of Cambodia. Paul shared with us that there were many students who were coming in from the rural provinces who did not have money to stay in dormitories. Most were finding a spot in Buddhist temples and sleeping there on the temple floor on small mats. When CNEC, Paul's ministry group, heard this, it became a burden on their hearts to buy or rent apartments to provide safe places for students from the provinces to stay. CNEC advertised at a variety of universities about free room and board. They would offer a place to sleep and free food in exchange for students attending Bible studies in the evenings for a few nights.

The weekend that we spent in Phomn Penh was such a delight! We met about 125 Khmer university students and joined in their time of worship in the evening. Most of the students had already given their lives to Christ. On Sunday, after the church service and lunch, three of the students asked if we would like to visit their museum. We couldn't imagine what was in a museum of this little country, but they seemed eager to show us, so we agreed to go with them. Off we went in a little tuktuk, with two students and Mesa, another student, driving this cute three-wheeled little vehicle. We definitely were not prepared for what we found. The museum was a former high school, famously known as S-21. I was horrified as we walked from classroom to classroom to see, vividly displayed, the horrors and atrocities committed in that school during the years of 1975-79 referred to as Khmer Rouge.

During those very same years, Lynn and I were serving in the country of Zimbabwe and were experiencing the atrocities of the war of independence there. We did not have a TV in Zimbabwe, and it was before internet, so we knew little about what was going on in the rest of the world.

Khmer Rouge started in the jungles of eastern Cambodia during the late 1960's. The movement gained momentum, and in 1975, their army gained enough strength to overthrow Phnom

Penh, the capital of Cambodia. Khmer Rouge gained notoriety as leading the worst mass killings of the 20th Century.

Pol Pot was the man who was the head of the regime that had its communist beginnings out in the rural areas of Cambodia. His plan was to take the people of Cambodia pretty much back to the Middle Ages. His agenda: to force millions who were living in the cities, and for sure anyone who was educated, to work in communal farm situations.

During that five-year period, whole families died either from execution, starvation, or disease. Pol Pot emptied the cities, abolished money and religion and set up small rural towns under his control. Anyone thought to be an intellectual (if they wore glasses, or were bilingual) was targeted. Because of the cruel tortures and deaths, family members often turned in their family members for self-preservation. Hundreds of thousands were tortured in the high school.

We found ourselves that sunny Sunday afternoon in the same building where atrocities had taken place. In our travels, we have visited Dachau in Germany and other similar places of torture and death, but for some reason this museum impacted me like no other. As we walked around the infamous high school where thousands upon thousands were tortured and died, we saw the documented faces of men and women and children, with numbers hanging around their necks to identify them. I could not hold back the tears. It was horrific! How could a human mind even conceive of the horrors that were done in that place?

Seeing the faces of those innocent people who had been tortured, each one standing before a camera with a number hanging around their neck to identify them before they were killed was appalling. Young people, older people, both men and women all faced absolutely horrible deaths. Their dull eyes were staring ahead blankly, knowing what they would endure. I felt they were looking into my very soul.

I learned a fact from a social worker. Often, after extreme trauma, a person or group often experiences what is called Flat Effect. Emotions are suppressed and hidden; the victims have no tears. After two and a half million of the six million people in one small nation are tortured and killed or let starve to death, one's mind cannot grasp the horror. The students who were with us had not seen these atrocities personally because they were too young, but many of them had lost parents, grandparents, aunts, and uncles, and as a result, their emotions were stunted.

The young university men who took us to the museum seemed almost puzzled by the depth of our emotions, as if we ourselves somehow were reliving the horror that the Khmer people faced. More than two and a half million people met horrific deaths, and we were standing in that museum with the sons and grandsons of the survivors. Even Hollywood was shocked at all that had happened in the country, and they attempted to capture the horror of it all, in a movie called "The Killing Fields."

***

As we left the museum, still stunned by all that we had seen, our young university hosts had something else on their minds. They asked if we enjoyed soccer. Lynn has played all of his life, so that was an easy answer: Yes! They asked if they could take us to their soccer game. We left the horrors of the S 21 torture center and headed to the joy and excitement of a full-blown soccer match. We were later to learn that these university students were using soccer as a way to reach out to other young men in the city of Phnom Penh and were having opportunities to share their faith in Jesus. How refreshing and life-giving after walking through the museum of horrors.

The young people that we met during those brief four days in Cambodia impacted our lives in such a huge way that when we were asked before we left the country, "Would you ever consider coming back to teach Bible and English in the dormitories?" we were quick to respond, "Yes!"

One of the young men that won our hearts on that first visit was Rathana Moeun. The first time we met him, he was playing soccer and the next day we met him at the Pillars Dormitory where he was serving as pastor.

Rathana's parents were among the thousands who had fled their native country of Cambodia and escaped to live in a refugee camp in Thailand near the Northern Cambodian border. They fled for safety and left almost everything that they had in Cambodia. Rathana was born while his parents were living in the Koa-I-Dang refugee camp in Northern Thailand.

Rathana leading prayer

The dictionary describes a refugee as a person who is forced to leave their country to escape war, persecution or natural disasters. Rathana's family escaped Cambodia via a dangerous route, so that their family could live in the safety of Thailand. I personally can't imagine what it would be like living displaced, in tents, crowded into areas with people that you had never met, with just a very small amount of your personal belongings. Rathana's family was there until he was six years old. The first six to seven years of a person's life can be the most impressionable. The Thailand refugee camp was a new norm for his family. It was not easy, but they were safer there than they had been in Cambodia.

When Rathana was almost seven, the camp was closed, and his parents decided to return to Cambodia. They settled in a town called Battambang. The Khmer Rouge was gone, driven from the country by the Vietnamese, and people were starting to return to their homes. But the new norm was perhaps harder than when they went to Thailand.

Those who had escaped Cambodia to go to Thailand, were discriminated against when they tried to return. They were not welcomed; they returned to their towns with nothing, because they had not been able to work in Thailand. Poverty was rampant. Rathana's family were now the poorest of the poor, and life was hard.

Rathana was able to attend school, but when he was around 11, he was introduced to Mormonism. It seemed appealing, and he was part of the Mormon group for about a year. Rathana then decided to quit, and he remembers turning his back completely on anything to do with God. Rathana applied for a government scholarship at the end of his 12th grade and was accepted for a program in Phnom Penh. His family had no money, so it was a real problem for him to find a place to live. He heard of the Crossroads dormitory where students were allowed to stay with free room and board, and he decided to move there, but with the determination not to believe anything about Jesus or His teachings.

Things were not easy for Rathana and at a very low point in his life, when he was questioning everything, he asked, "How can a Christian live with joy in the midst of crisis? Is that even possible or is it delusional?"

Trying to find the answers to these questions, he decided to engage in singing and studying during the evening times of worship at Crossroads dormitory. One night, through a dream, God used Isaiah 6:8 to speak to Rathana: *"Who will go for me, whom shall I send?"*

Rathana felt that God was speaking directly to him. He was no longer the refugee, running from God. God has had an amazing plan for this young man. Rathana recognized that he was called specifically to do God's will, and he became a dedicated Christ follower. Later the church commissioned him to be a church planter.

What a joy it has been to watch Rathana on this journey. He was selected as one to leave Cambodia again, this time not running away from, but running toward something bigger. He was given the opportunity to go to seminary in Manilla. He spent four years studying completely in English and earned his Master's in Divinity degree, graduating with honors. Presently, Rathana is the pastor of the church in Phnom Penh where he is teaching others to be followers of Jesus. How amazing it has been to watch the journey of one whose life has been transformed. God has healed his heart. By restoring the hope that the refugee camps had taken away, God was preparing Rathana for this time. Now he is sharing what he learned with others.

37

From Dreamer to Doctor
Cambodia

In January of 2011, on our first visit to Cambodia, we spent time with a young man named Vuthea. Vuthea had plans to become a doctor and was in the pre-med program at the University. At the time he was 23 years old but looked even younger.

Vuthea's background was a challenging one. He was one of 14 children. When he was 12 years old, he was taken from his home and sent to live with "an organization." While there, he was the victim of sexual abuse from both men and women.

After coming to Christ, his life was truly transformed. The lack of trust that he had in people had been replaced by a joy that was truly contagious. The frown of worry and concern that had been on his face when we first met was replaced by an infectious smile. The joy in his heart spread to all those around him. He was the go-to man whenever anyone in our group was sick.

The building where I lived during my one-month stay each January housed the main office, the Worship Center, and the men's dormitory. There were a few guest rooms and mine became known as "Grandma's room." The getaway place in the three-story building was the flat, open roof. It was a place where we squatted on our haunches and did our laundry in buckets. After using the hose to get everything well rinsed, we would hang the clothes over the wires at the side of the roof. There were also a few tables and chairs for the students to study and do homework. Most importantly it was a place of semi quiet, far above the noise of the constant, heavy, traffic in the streets of Phnom Penh. For the most part it was quiet. Occasionally the sounds of the street vendors selling their wares drifted up to our level. Horns were always beeping from motorbikes or trucks or cars that were attempting to pass one another on the narrow, single-lane streets, trying to decide who had the right of way.

When I returned in 2012, and went upstairs to the roof, I found it absolutely transformed. Where it had been refreshing and nice, but certainly a dull gray, now it was like a garden! There were bright colored bougainvillea bushes in various spots around the roof and tall palm plants waving their branches. There was an abundance of flower pots that blended in with the greenery and bordering the circumference of the roof. I noticed that a wire grid had been meticulously woven across the ceiling. When I asked about it, I was told that it was to discourage the doves and other birds from making their nests in the rafters and eventually "dirtying" the floors.

I wondered how this had all come about. I discovered that, in addition to his vigorous pre-med program, Vuthea had decided he would like to beautify the roof. It was an amazing transformation. I also wondered why he was spending so much of his own money to make this place so beautiful. One morning, I was up reading my Bible and praying, and he was there watering all the flowers and plants, so I asked him.

Vuthea's reply, "I want this place to become a place of beauty and rest for all of our students, but also so that people who are not Christ followers would want to come and spend time here so we can find a way to tell them about Jesus."

Each day I spent there, I was surprised and humbled by the concern and commitment of these young Cambodian students to find practical ways to carry out the Great Commission: go and teach and make disciples of all they meet.

Judy with Vuthea and another student

I was totally blown away by their interest in horticulture and beautification, and I told the young men who were working on all of this that I would love to help. Our daughter had recently moved to a farm, and she loved plants and flowers. When I wrote and told her about the beautification project on the roof she said, "Mom, our family would love to be involved in this. Please spend $50 the next time they go out and buy some plants from us." Our sending church wrote that they would like to be involved, so a plan was made that we would go shopping together and purchase a few more tables and chairs to place around this roof-top sanctuary.

On a Saturday morning we decided to go plant and table shopping. They were university students, so I thought they surely would sleep in a little bit. I was only two days in country, so the 13-hour time difference and jet lag had me a little upside down. But very, very early that Saturday morning there was a knock on the door, "Will you be ready soon, Grandma?"

Wanting to grab a quick shower before we went, I told them I would be ready soon. Showering in Cambodia always made me giggle. The little shower in my room is sort of a combined toilet and shower all in one. When you turn on the shower head, everything in the whole little room gets wet, toilet paper and all! And I would smile to myself, as I sleepily turned on the water, standing a little bit away from the shower head. The water was ice cold. I kept my hand under the water faucet, eyes closed, catching the last few winks of sleep, but waiting for the water to warm up a bit. I kept waiting and waiting for the cold stream to get hot, or even lukewarm. Then I remembered, it is never going to get hot or lukewarm, there was no water heater. I had a very quick shower, and we were soon ready to get on the road.

Five of us headed out in the little tuk tuk, the special mode of transportation in Phnom Penh. A tuk tuk is three-wheeled vehicle like a motor bike with a little cart in the back that would seat four. One of the guys rode alongside us on a motorbike to where the flowers and plants were sold. One whole section of town is dedicated to horticulture. The guys were super picky: What colors should we have? What plants stand up to the heat? But most importantly, they knew the money was a gift, and they wanted to choose wisely. After four, yes, I mean *four* hours of shopping, we finally drove away with three orchids, a water lily and six other colorful plants. The kids were ecstatic.

When we got back, they went right up to the roof to plant, and I went to the little kitchen to do some baking. While I was baking, I heard a slushing sound in the bathroom, where I found a muddy, yucky waterfall coming over the steps out of the bathroom. Did I mention YUCK? It was gross and smelly. I quickly ran to the dormitories to call for reinforcements among the students, and they came like a shot. We all spent the next hour or so mopping up all the bathrooms on the three floors. We went by motorbike to the local market to try to find bleach and disinfectant.

What had caused the problem? After waiting for a plumber and having the water turned off for the rest of the day, it was discovered that in the process of beautification, a mistake was made. The guys wanted the roof perfect. They swept it so clean, and swept all the leaves, twigs and dirt into the corner of the roof, and all of that went down the drain pipe. The drain could only take so much, and it became totally clogged from the bottom floor all the way up to the roof and then spillage and destruction followed. The pipes cracked and each floor was a total mess.

What a great illustration for my time of teaching that night. Sometimes when we are trying to make everything "look good," we just bury things. Instead of dealing with things in our life that should be dealt with, we let them clog up our life and never are truly honest with God. It was a poignant lesson for us all—very real and very applicable as we all had spent the day without water because of not dealing with the things that clog the pipes. How important it is for us also to have the flood gates open between us and God.

***

For some time, the students had wanted to reach out to a group called the Kuy. The Kuy spoke their own language and knew very little Khmer, the language of the people of Cambodia. The students heard about this unreached people and had done research on them. The Kuy people lived quite primitively, getting their water from wells and having no electricity in the village. After several months of praying for this endeavor, the students had gone to visit the village, and they continued to make the seven-hour trip every few months.

The model that the students were following was one that came about in cross-cultural ministries in early 2010. In 2012, the book Miraculous Movements pushed this idea into the minds of literally thousands of gospel workers. The author of this book writes:

> "Jesus commanded His disciples to seek out a person of peace whenever they entered a new community. In this process, two things should connect. First, the person of peace is waiting for someone to help him deal with a significant spiritual hunger... Second, the church planter or disciple maker must be looking for the person of peace." (Miraculous Movements by Jerry Trousdale, pg. 95).

The main focus of Vuthea's life is medicine, and he continued to study hard. But there was also a deep, spiritual side of him that was tender. God often revealed things to him through dreams.

Vuthea had never been to the village, and the night before he left for the journey, he had a dream of a specific man, living in a specific house in that far-off village that he had never even been to. After the long trip, the students arrived and freshened up, and started to walk to different homes along the road. Vuthea, without ever having been to this village, went directly to the house that God had shown him in his dream. The man was at home, sitting in his house that was made of wooden slats which was built up on stilts.

The first thing that Vuthea discovered was that the man in his dream was the local sorcerer--the witch doctor. After several hours of discussion with him, Vuthea had the privilege of sharing the message of the Gospel with this man. The witch doctor made a decision to become a Christ follower. God has had His hand on Vuthea. And so began the work in that very remote village.

***

I had a sleepover with some of the lady students in one of the dorms across town. In the morning, the girls went off to school, and the young pastor offered to drive me back to my room at the office on his motor bike. He is one of the kindest young men I have met. As we were driving, he said, "Grandma, do you eat bread for breakfast in America?"

I had to think for a few seconds, *Oh! he must mean toast* I thought, so I responded "Yes, we eat bread."

He said, "I would like to treat you to breakfast." I appreciated his thoughtfulness.

Before long we pulled over to a road-side stand, and the pastor got off the motorbike. I was a little surprised because I didn't see any toasters. He walked up to the stand and put in an order.

I have a somewhat weird sense of humor, but as I sat there on the back of his motorbike, waiting for him to return, I noticed a lady sitting right in front of the motorbike, washing lettuce in the stream of water coming down the street. I thought to myself, *"I rarely get sick, but I have a feeling if ever I do, it will be right here."*

I started taking photos of the lady washing the lettuce and the roadside stand and the surroundings. I just knew this would be a prime time for a tummy bug. I also watched the lady at the stand spread some mystery sauce on a piece of bread, and top it with the lettuce that had been cleaned in the river. Meat was placed on top of that and covered with another piece of bread.

The young pastor came back, handed me the plastic bag, and hopped on the bike to head back to the dorm. What a dear. He was so kind and he was treating Grandma with what he assumed was going to be an American breakfast. Meanwhile, I had taken four or five photos of what I was pretty sure I would call, "The day I got sick in Cambodia."

We went back to the dorm, got two glasses of water and sat down to eat our breakfast. We were about half-way through the sandwich and my friend said, "I don't think I can finish mine." A Khmer breakfast usually consisted of noodles or rice soup, not this exotic bread and mystery sauce. I didn't finish mine either.

I was supposed to take three of the students out for pizza that night to celebrate the birthday of one of the boys, but by 3 PM, I was feeling quite bilious. I didn't want to cancel the birthday party, but when we arrived, I knew my predictions were spot-on. The thought of food was unappealing. I made it through the birthday celebration, having the occasional sip of Coke, but then I hurried back to the dorm. I am pretty sure that not even through four pregnancies with bad morning sickness, had I ever experienced a cleansing like this! I was up all night and thought that death would be a welcome reprieve. I had to cancel my trip to the rural Kuy village the next day.

The Khmer way of soothing people was massage. The girls are amazingly lovely and thoughtful and when word was out that I was sick, I often had four Khmer girls sitting on either side of me, giving me a massage pretty much all day. It was little awkward for quick exits to the bathroom, but their love was so soothing.

Then Vuthea, almost a doctor, got word that I was sick and came to my room. He decided that I had food poisoning (I think that my photo journal had predicted that the day before). He went out and came back a while later with antibiotics that he was going to administer intravenously. He was a second-year pre-med student; what could possibly go wrong? He told me he would let it drip slowly to be sure that I was not allergic to the antibiotics. We sat together for about twenty minutes chatting until it was all inside me and good.

That night Vuthea became my primary care doctor. He came to the door around 10 PM and shared with me that he felt I needed another IV bag of fluids to replace all that I had lost. He brought in another IV drip and hooked it up to my left arm. We had nowhere to hang the bag, so he asked if I would lie at the foot of the bed so he could hang the IV bag from my closet door handle. I did that. He amazingly and kindly offered to sleep on the floor all night to make sure I was okay, but I was already beginning to feel so much better that I convinced him to go back to his room and get a good night's sleep.

My arm was getting tired from being elevated and leaning on the wooden footboard. Even though I was tired, I knew that I would never fall asleep in that position, so I needed to come up with a plan.

I always bring an Ambien (those tiny little sleeping aids) for my arrival night in Cambodia to help me get over the jet lag, and then I save one for when I return to the States for the 24-hour trip. It can put me asleep in just minutes, and sure enough, it did the trick that night.

My sleep was so deep that I forgot about the drip in my arm, and I cozied down into a fetal position at the end of the bed, curled up with my arms under my face. Vuthea came in and checked on me a 4 AM and he was horrified. He had only a little flashlight to check on me. Suddenly, the overhead lights in my room were blazing and a horrified Vuthea was frantic. Apparently, in the process of getting cozy, I bent my arm and the needle bent as well. When the needle bent, I bled some, and the whole IV bag of fluid spilled out, making my sheets look like I had bled out. Poor, poor Vuthea!

I was in my delightful ambient-induced sleep and could hear, as if I was in a well, a voice calling, "Grandma, Grandma."

I was having a hard time waking myself up. Finally, I smiled at Vuthea, and I remember saying, "Good job, Vuthea; I am feeling great. But why are you here in the middle of the night?" The color returned to his face, and we both had a big smile as he removed the IV from my arm.

Vuthea and I are still in touch by Facebook, and recently we were remembering this time. He wrote, "Grandma, I was sure you were dead because I couldn't wake you." Ambien does that to me. Yummy sleep, though.

I remember that experience with such love and gratitude. I would not change it for anything. I knew that for all the pain in my tummy, I would never, ever have traded those couple of days. The young man who wanted so much to please me and buy an American breakfast; Vuthea finding antibiotic for an IV and then the IV to replace my lost fluids, Vuthea taking such good care of me, and the abundant love of these girls who took shifts giving me soothing massages: it all made me feel like a princess and ever so blessed.

Looking back, I wonder sometimes, did I imagine all of that? This very day, ten years after that trip, I sent a message to Dr. Vuthea. He finished pre-med; he applied for a scholarship to Med school in Paris; and he is now a plastic surgeon back in Phnom Penh. I asked him again, "Do you remember when you took care of me when I got food poisoning?"

He responded, "When you were so sick, I was scared to death. I saw the blood all over your sheet, and I thought that I killed you. But that experience has made me more careful with each patient I have ever had."

He also said, "I am so appreciative to God for all my difficulties in my early life because each one was a lesson that He was teaching me. He has led me all the way and stayed by my side." What an encouragement and blessing to be reminded of God's faithfulness by this man who had such a rough young life. He met the Healer and his life was turned around.

There are now stories of Khmer people whose parents had suffered atrocities but who have turned to God and trust Him. We all have choices. Vuthea's choice was either to be a victim of a terrible childhood or to see God in the midst and submit to being refined by Him to be a victor. Knowing his story has helped me to grow in my faith.

38

Uncle Hun
The Kuy Village

On my second trip to Cambodia, I had the privilege to travel with Pastor Chris Hardy and Rebecca Pittard, who were on staff at Westover church. We would be spending two weeks with the students of the Bible college to do leadership training.

It was September and the monsoon season. The students of the Crossroads church with whom we had been working, had a vision of going to this totally new area to start a church.

The Kuy were a people group who settled in Cambodia, Laos and Thailand. They spoke a language unique to them. Our entourage of students drove in two trucks and motorbikes and stopped half way for a break and some snacks. We were urged to try some of the local snacks. It was my first time to try BBQ tarantula, fried crickets and some other tasty morsels. We traveled a few hours more and drove to a small town nearest to our destination at the Kuy village and left the trucks there. During the monsoons, it was impossible to get cars or trucks into their village.

After putting big sacks of rice and vegetables in an oxcart, which was the only thing capable of traversing the muddy roads, we were ready to go. My dear friend, Rebecca, and I were given seats of honor on top of the sacks of rice in the oxcart. During the whole trip, we were constantly treated with such care and respect, being the older women. As we were trundling along in the cart, attempting to keep our balance, we could see the sky beginning to get very black and the clouds moving in our direction. A torrential rain, unlike anything I had seen, started, and in a matter of minutes, we were all drenched. We saw one of the student leaders running towards us carrying a tarp. At that point, we were sure that we were being treated like Princesses, and assumed they wanted to cover us from the rain. Alas, that was not their plan!

"Get out, get out," called Potra. "We need to cover the rice." Rebecca and I had a humbling laugh at our quick removal, and we walked the last few miles with everyone else in the pouring rain.

Arriving in the village was like a return to Africa. There was no electricity, only a well for water, and one little outhouse. It was placed across the field and up the hill quite a ways from the houses on stilts. The weekend was such an amazing treat. I think that I was made for third world living. However, the learning curve was big.

All the students were very prepared; they showered and changed into warm, dry clothes. We had packed light and didn't have a lot of options. The sun was soon out and the heat dried us out pretty quickly. However, it was good for us to observe the showering process so we would know how to do it when it was our turn.

There was a little grass shelter at the edge of the property near the well. We were somewhat taller than the Khmer people, so the grass shelter did not quite reach the top of our heads. We observed people going to the well and fetching buckets of water. We were getting the idea. When it was time for me and Rebecca to shower, we decided to go in together, and we forgot the process. As soon as we got in the little grass shelter, a sweet voice called, "Grandma, here is the water for you." How could we have forgotten? Someone kindly had gone to the well and brought us two buckets of water.

The same was true as we would walk through the field with the cows and goats up to the outhouse. It was a cute little building. The hook to keep the door closed was on the outside, so Rebecca and I always went together so one of us could lock it. How many times did we make the trip there, and once again, hear someone calling, "Grandma, here is some water for you." Some dear soul had seen us walking in that direction and realized we were bucketless and helped us out.

Uncle Hun was a man of peace. (Luke 10:6) Although he could not read anything else, he was learning to read the Bible. He was the first in his village to be saved. The village built their church on his property.

The Kuy people were welcoming. After we shared rice on Friday night, someone started playing music. I am not a dancer, but the ladies were doing some dances to local music, so I joined in. Although we couldn't communicate in words, we laughed and danced and had a wonderful time together. After all the frivolity with the ladies, the men sitting around talking, and the students having a special story time and singing and games with the kids, it was time to go to sleep.

The students all had nifty little sleeping bags that they hung all under the house on stilts. They had mosquito gauze over the top, so they zipped themselves in and were quickly asleep. Chris, Rebecca, and I were given the place of honor to sleep, up in the house with Uncle Hun, his wife and all the children. Mats were laid over the wooden slats, and we each had a blanket, and a big mosquito net covered all three of us. The slats of the floor were not close together, so it was pretty easy to see the ground below, as well as hear the roosters and chickens and cows in the field behind us. Obviously, with no electricity there is not a television, but that night we felt like we were the featured show. This was the first time that foreigners had been to their village, no less sleeping in their home. The children turned the lamps facing us, so we were sort of on stage under the lights thus, we decided to just sleep in our clothes. The wooden slats with the gaps between took a little getting used to, but we finally settled down and the lamps were turned off.

The dark sky and the brilliant stars were breathtaking. However, having to use the outhouse in the middle of the night proved to be a little challenging. I had to get out of from under the large mosquito net quietly, tiptoe so as not to wake all the children, climb down the pole-steps ladder, then walk through the field to get to the outhouse. The second night Rebecca and I decided no more drinking after 2 PM so we could avoid those late-night walks through the field.

Saturday was an amazing day when I learned to make Khmer rice noodles. We learned that day that it definitely takes a village to make Khmer noodles. All of the local women gathered together at one of the homes. The rice had been soaking overnight and now was of a pasty consistency. Pots were filled with water and set to boil as the rice paste got thicker and thicker. Then came the hard work of kneading. There were about five ladies "assigned" to kneading.

I got to do all the jobs as they were trying to show me the whole process. Mesa, one of the leaders, was always by my side as interpreter/cultural helper and through the years, he became like a son. He did the unusual for me–helped with the women's work! The ladies loved it! He is funny and helpful. When it was my turn to knead, and I was thinking that I was doing great, the ladies were shaking their heads…I needed more water! One of them threw a big handful that she had dipped from the pot of water, and I didn't realize it was boiling water. That caused an outbreak of laughter as I cringed at the burning sensation. Another bonding moment with these sweet, hard-working women.

After a bunch of dough was kneaded sufficiently, we started the fun part. They had a contraption made of tin. At the bottom, they had hammered holes in the metal in a beautiful pattern. A large tree trunk, like a see saw, was placed over the fire as one lady put a big chunk of the rice dough in the container. Another lady sat on the tree trunk, squeezing the rice mixture which was now looking like noodles, through the tin into the boiling water.

The noodles cooked for a while and another lady pulled them off the fire, and the process was repeated.

That night was such joy! The whole village gathered, and we shared the noodles together. We were there only three days, but the dancing and singing, the noodle making, and the visits in homes were such blessings. Then came Sunday, the day of worship and the baptisms of those who had made the decision to become Christ followers. What a special day.

The witch doctor Vuthea had shared with, Uncle Hun, was there to be baptized and there were about 20 others. A small net was placed in the water to keep the leeches away from those who were doing the baptisms.

Uncle Hun, who often contacts me on Facebook

I wear toe rings and a teenage girl and her mom were admiring them. I took them off and gave each of them one. Words are not always needed to communicate. A smile, kneading together; dancing together, laughing together or crying together, giving gifts; where there are no words, God provides a way to communicate.

As I left Uncle Hun's village that first trip, I knew that their faces and smiles and love would be part of me forever. The weekend had been full. We learned a lot. We made many new friends, people with whom we could not speak to with words, but with whom our hearts were bound together.

Since then, each January that I spent in Cambodia, I have had the privilege of renewing friendships with the people of Uncle Hun's village. As of this writing, it has been ten years since that weekend, and a few months ago I received a "friend request" on Facebook. It was Uncle Hun. I can't quite figure out how that works in a village with no electricity except car batteries. But we are now Facebook buddies. We still can't speak each other's language, but we share emojis and photos of one another's grandkids, like all grandparents do.

Uncle Hun and the people of his village are treasures in my heart and connections that are long lasting. The things I learned were not work-related, but heart-related. God works in beautiful, mysterious ways.

39

Phearak - From Buddhist
to Christian

Phearak came to Phnom Penh as a freshman at the university. He was from a practicing Buddhist home, like almost everyone in Cambodia. He had heard about the dormitories of the Crossroads Church and applied to stay there. There are so many young people who come in from the provinces but have no place to stay, so they stay on the floors of Buddhist temples. Crossroads Ministries rents homes and provides places where university students can stay with free room and board. The only commitment is that they are asked to attend the evening Bible studies for four nights a week. Phearak agreed to do that, and after a surprisingly short time of living in the dorm, he gave his life to God and was excited about the journey that he had before him.

Shortly after he made that commitment to God, he came up with an amazing plan for his future to make his life count for God. Part of that plan was to return to his province on his next vacation and share the peace that he had found in God with his Buddhist parents. There is no doubt in the Khmer culture that parents are honored and respected. He loved them so much that now that he had this relationship with God, he wanted to share it with his parents. On his first two visits home, he was met with

Phearak

rejection; the family had no interest in leaving the Buddhist faith. They wanted nothing to do with his newfound faith in God.

For about seven years, I stayed for the month of January in the dormitory, teaching English and Bible to the university students. Phearak was in my English class, and he asked me to pray for his upcoming visit back to his home when he planned to share again his love for God with his parents. By this third visit back to share, his parents commented on the consistent joy and love that they were seeing in him. He was living out his faith–not necessarily with words. They saw the changes in his life and finally asked him how they too could find out more about God.

The following January when I was there, he told me his parents were coming in from the province and that I would get to meet them. They were now Christ followers, growing in their faith. They spent the night and joined us for church. It was so precious to see this family whose lives had turned to love for

God; it was so evident. It was also such an encouragement to the students who also were praying for their parents. The joy on the faces of Phearak's family and the testimonies that they shared in church of God's faithfulness were such a blessing to us all. After the church service, all of the students wanted to go up to the roof and take a "family photo." Their prayers for Phearak's family had been answered, and we were all rejoicing.

***

The next morning, I was up on the roof of our building very early reading my Bible. Phearak's little brother was also up there, and he seemed absolutely enthralled with everything he could find on the roof. He was flitting around like a butterfly, checking every flower and plant. He was trying to catch pigeons, and he seemed enthralled with our decorated roof garden. He found a hive of bees and although we had never met, and could not speak each other's language, with each new "find," he would rush over to me, take my hand, and pull me towards his discovery. I immediately fell in love with this dear boy and even ran down to my room to get my camera to attempt to capture his joy and enthusiasm. Even with my camera, it was impossible to capture! It was very rare to find an entire family of Christ followers in Cambodia. Seeing this family of four, who were so in love with Jesus, truly impacted my heart.

Making a trip in from the province is not always easy, but they had come to town to pick up Grandpa, who was flying in from Australia. Grandma had been tortured and killed back during the time of Khmer Rouge, and Grandpa had fled the country. He was a High Priest in the Buddhist temple. He was returning to Cambodia for two reasons: First and foremost, it was a time of remembrance of his wife's death many years before. Second, and maybe equally as important to him, he was coming to get Phearak and his younger brothers enrolled in a monastery so that they could become Buddhist Monks and follow in Grandpa's footsteps. When Phearak shared that with us, the whole Crossroads church started praying. It became a primary prayer for all of the students that Phearak and his brothers could be spared that. Grandparents have a huge impact in the life of the children and grandchildren, so all of our prayers were very specific in regards to the boys.

A few days after the parents' visit, I had an extremely busy day: a 5:30 am walk at the Olympic stadium with two of the girls, breakfast with several students, two classes, lunch and just lots of people activities, which I loved. The Khmer ladies are so loving. I often felt as though I had Velcro on my arms. Everywhere I would go, there was always someone very closely attached and extremely protective. The elderly people are highly respected and cared for in the Cambodian culture.

The gate to our property had a big chain and lock keeping the motorbikes and students safe. If I attempted to go alone out the gate to the street outside our office, the chain rattled and invariably someone would just appear, like a genie out of a bottle. "Where are you going, Grandma?" I was asked.

"Just for a walk" or to the store or to one of the other dorms.

"By yourself?" That was just not acceptable! Someone would always walk with me, no matter what they were doing. They would stop studying or watching soccer on TV and accompany me. As if a silent alarm had sounded, even if they were really busy, someone would just appear. I am an extrovert, so having someone with me from the time I came out of my room in the morning till when I went to bed in the evening was okay with me.

This particular day, there was a lag in activities and I decided to go upstairs and check my texts. There was a message from Phearak. His text was pretty much my undoing.

Phearak and I had connected deeply in our English class together. One day we were talking about names, and he asked what people back in the United States called me.

"Well, it depends. Officially my name is Judith Ann; most friends call me Judy; really close friends call me Jud; my precious family calls me Mom; some of my grandkids call me

Grandma, but the younger grandkids call me Gigi; in Africa I am called Gogo. In Phnom Penh five of the older students that I met when I first visited call me Mom, and the rest called me Grandma." I never thought anything of this conversation again until I saw this text message from him that busy afternoon.

"Gigi, I won't be at English class today. I am so sorry to miss it. My grandfather made me come to talk to him. Do you remember he just came from Australia and he is a High Priest at the Buddhist Pagoda? Please Gigi, would you pray? He has taken my two brothers and enrolled them into the monastery to be Buddhist monks, and he wants me to come enter as well."

What? The precious, joyful, bouncing ten-year-old, Phear-ak's little brother, filled with the joy of the Lord, was now going to spend his life as a monk and live in a monastery? Grand-father wants Phearak to join?

I was incredulous. Hadn't we been praying for him every day since the grandfather had arrived, asking God NOT to let this happen? My heart was broken. I went up to the roof. There had always been someone there with whom I could talk and pray, but this time there was no one.

I called over the edge of the roof down to the third-floor boys' dorm to find some guys to come up and pray with me. NO ONE!!!

I phoned Vuthea, one of the students. He had just driven me to the store, so I knew that he had to be home. He didn't answer so I texted and asked him, if he were home, to please come up and pray with me and just talk to God about changing the grandpa's heart. He returned my call pretty quickly: "Oh, Grandma, I just left to teach an English class at the orphanage. Can I come and pray with you tonight after Bible study?"

God was there, of course! I talked, and He listened. Yes, He comforted me, but for the first time in all my months and years of visiting Phnom Penh, I felt really alone. There was no one around Velcroed to my arm. I just wanted to be part of the "two or three gathered in His name" to pray for protection for that dear young boy and Phearak. I had heard stories from some of the students about the monasteries–the abuse and other things that went on–and I my heart was aching.

I finally got my keys and walked down the road to the women's dorm. I would normally not have been permitted to walk there alone, but I did and was so thankful to find three of the lady students at home studying. I shared Phearak's text with them. Phearak was so well-loved by all the students; we had all been praying for his family.

As was the case so many times, the students did the ministering to me, the pastor's wife. It was a precious time with all of us, crying out to God for his protection and intervention. God's peace came upon us. This situation didn't take God by surprise. God never says, "Whoops." We reminded one another of God's sovereignty. We truly felt the presence of God in our midst that day. The girls started to walk me back to the office and up to my room. Having them minister to me was such a gift. All that they learned about God and prayer and His will came flooding over me, as this time, I was the one wavering. What a gift to see their love and their knowledge of Scripture flow out towards me.

As we were walking back to my office, my phone buzzed. It was Vichetra, one of the leaders at Crossroads. "Mom, Vuthea called me a while ago and said to find you, that you are hurting. I left work a little early, and I even found a Coke Zero (hard to find in PP, but he knew it was my favorite). I will be at home by the time you get there, and I will be waiting on the roof to talk and pray."

***

It doesn't matter if the elder is teaching the younger or the younger is ministering to the older. We are One Body. When one hurts, we all hurt. That night we started our Bible study with a time of prayer. There were 85 university students, deeply concerned and praying for those precious young boys. The grandfather gave up on Phearak entering the monastery, and we were thankful. His younger brother did not miraculously get out of the monastery, but I believe with all my heart that God has protected him there through the years.

How thankful I am that I am a part of this Body of Christ–to pray with, encourage, and be encouraged.

40

The River City

Shortly after we returned from Africa in 1983, Lynn took on his new responsibilities as an Area Director for West Asia. His first overseas trip was spending three weeks in India. Never one to be overly emotional, when he returned, he sat with me at breakfast and wept at the oppression he had found in the country. "Judy, they have 330 million gods. Most are made of stone or some inanimate object. How will the people of India ever hear about the love of God?"

The city that he spent most of his time in is one of the holiest of Hindu cities. It is believed to be 5000 years old and one of the oldest places where people have been living constantly all those years. Daily, thousands of people come by train, car, and plane to worship at the Ghats (the stairs leading up from the Ganges River into the city). These are the places where the people go to worship at sunset. At sunrise, at those same stairs, they do puja (worship) and bathe in the Ganges, considered to be holy water. Older people spend time close to the river, hoping that, when they are close to death, someone will pour holy water from the river in their mouth so they can be reborn to a higher or better state in the next life. There are approximately 88 Ghats in the city. Most Hindu people want to be cremated at the Ghats and have their ashes sent out on a barge to be dispersed in the river.

The Ghats on the Ganges

The idolatry in the city felt like a hot, wet blanket. People worship stone gods, and trees, and just about anything to which they can ascribe holiness. There are hundreds of thousands of stone idols; people do pilgrimages to them to earn their way to heaven. Every time Lynn returned from a trip to that city, his heart was so concerned.

That particular city is also known as the graveyard of Christian workers; discouragement and obstacles overcome them. It was just outside this city that Buddha began teaching followers under a banyan tree. Buddhism was born there, then spread to other East Asian countries.

Thirty years after his first visit to the river city, Lynn and I were able to visit workers who were being supported by our church and who had been working there for several years. In the process of visiting them, we met an unusually gifted couple and their two daughters. Martin is Indian and a Brahman, the highest caste in Indian culture. Louise is a woman from South Africa who went to serve in India with a team of other teachers. God put the two of them together, and they are still ministering in that river city which had broken Lynn's heart.

This dear couple, Martin and Louise, had a heart to work with the rail children of the city. Most of the kids come from the slums. Some are orphans; others have one or two parents living in abject poverty. I had seen the movie, "Slumdog Millionaire" and could not believe the plight of the children in that movie. Then I saw it for myself. Most of the children slept on the train station platforms. They tried to sell bottles of water when the trains would stop at their station. They would scramble on to the train when it stopped to let off or pick up passengers and try to find left over sandwiches or pieces of cookies—anything they could eat. Martin's heart was moved to compassion as he became aware of what was going on. That compassion, in itself, was a miracle. Most of the kids were of the Dalit caste, the untouchables—people with whom Martin's caste would traditionally have no interaction.

The couple found a piece of property for rent and began reno-

Martin and Louise

vate it. Through the years, each time we would visit, there was more progress on the renovations. Patches of grass were carried in from other locations, planted on the property, and watered lovingly. The lawn was like a piece of heaven for the kids who spent the majority of their lives on hot, dry, cement; they rarely had grass on which to play ball or have a picnic. Martin started meeting with the kids at the rail station, and he began building friendships. After trust and relationships were built, he began inviting them to the property he was renting, where he would serve chai, Indian tea with milk and sugar, as well as slices of buttered bread; refreshments that could at least help fill their empty stomachs.

The treats filled their stomachs and the trust between Martin and the kids began to grow deeper. Many of the children were victims of abuse so establishing trust took a long time. As time went by, and the property was being developed, Martin was able to build on parts of the property. He made classrooms for studying; he also started building a team of workers to help and teach. Many of the kids had addictions to "white out," the white fluid used for making corrections on typed paper. Some had mental confusion from their sniffing it. Others had sexual diseases from the abuse they suffered. Martin invited a doctor to visit once a month, and he was willing to do it pro bono. That was a wonderful help to the kids' well-being.

Their dream grew bigger; soon sewing classes were established for the girls so that they would have a marketable skill as they got older. Sewing machines were donated so the girls could make clothes for themselves, and they made and sold crafts.

Game time was always a favorite. Playing soccer or cricket in the cool grass when the temperature rose to well over 100 was a treat. They met several times a week, and after the food and games, there was time for telling Bible stories and singing. Martin would even pray with each of the kids.

Martin displayed a kindness that was almost unheard of to these kids. He became like the mayor of the area. In spite of the violence and despair in the slum areas, Martin was respected and trusted. Parents began to request guidance from him, and he held an honored place in the community.

Martin was concerned about these kids' futures. Being an entrepreneur at heart, he conceived a plan. Throughout the entire city of four million people there was not one laundry service or dry cleaner. Wealthier people would hire someone to wash their clothes in the Ganges, the holy river. They would beat the items against the rocks. The wear and tear on clothes were unbelievable. Many of the women wore Sari's made of the most gorgeous and delicate colorful silk that did not stand up well to being beaten against the rocks.

Martin presented his ideas to the Business as Mission team at our church. Business men, gifted with marketing skills and in writing business plans, came alongside Martin and helped him get started. They didn't invest money, but they spent hundreds of hours doing surveys, developing marketing ideas, strategizing on video calls, and designing logos to help Martin fulfill his dream of creating a way for those boys to learn a trade, get jobs, break the cycle of poverty, and get a new start in life. Foremost on Martin's heart was focusing on God. With millions of gods available to all Indians, Martin wanted to introduce them to the Living God.

We were impressed by the humility shown by Martin and Louise, working in such a hard place and doing it with great joy. The laundromat has now been expanded to include a dry cleaner where those beautiful silk Sari's could be cared for. Income from the business helped the kids with food, rent and books for classes. Martin discovered that many of those young people, despite their desperately poor environment, are very intelligent. His next dream: getting some of the children into schools, paying their school fees, and getting them books.

***

On one of our trips, we visited in the tiny tent home of two of the girls living in the slums. The shelter was small with no floor, just mud; imagine what it is like during the monsoon season. I have no idea how the two girls kept their uniforms cleaned and ironed, which was needed to attend the school. When we visited them, Martin pointed out the small steamer locker in the center of their shelter. He said that he had to buy that to keep their uniforms safe, because as the girls would eat their rice and lentils, if they could get any, the rats would come up and eat off their plates while they were eating. The locker was used as a table, but it was also the place where their school uniform and books could be kept safer from the weather and the rats.

Martin lived in the city with his lovely wife Louise and their two daughters, but their life was not without its sacrifices. Their faithfulness is a refreshing aroma of the God whom they serve. Their lives are such a testimony of joy and peace in serving.

We recently were able to make a visit there with a pastor from our new church in Texas. As our plans were coming together, our two eldest children heard where we were going. Both are on staff at two different churches and each came separately to Lynn, saying almost the exact same thing. "We have heard you talk about this city since we were teens. Is there any way I could travel with you both and experience what we have heard you talk about for so many years?"

It was very special for us to be able to travel with them both: to walk the streets and experience the sea of humanity rushing down to the Ghats for evening worship; to do a sunrise boat ride on what is considered their holy river; and to do Puja along with the hundreds of people bathing or washing their clothes. Cows rule the cities; everyone has to drive or move around them. They defecate where they please, and it is up to those walking to avoid the cowpies left everywhere. We walked among the burning ghats where scores of bodies were lined up to be cremated. Pictures don't do justice because they do not capture the smells, the deafening noise of people, cars, and motorbikes, and the ever-present sacred cows that can't be touched.

Our cries and prayers as we leave any country are always the same.

How will they hear?
How will they know?
Who will go?

41

A Grandma's Heart
for the Next Generation

When a couple makes a decision to travel overseas with their family to give themselves completely to serving God, the usual response of the missions-pastor's wife is excitement, joy, and thankfulness. Those were certainly my usual feelings. What a joy it is for me to cheer them on!

I can remember one exception in our ministry when I was hesitant to be that cheerleader. The couple we met were wonderful; they were not from our church but were introduced to us by the pastor of their home church. We loved and appreciated them at our very first meeting. Their enthusiasm and commitment to the task before them was amazing. The goal that they had set before them was certainly a needed one: to translate God's Word into the language of a culture that did not have a Bible. They were going to Iraq.

The couple had five children, like we did when we had served in Africa. Their plan was to take those five precious children ages eleven, eight, seven, five and three years old to settle in a hard and dusty place, a land with a lot of conflict. The history of the country was filled with strife. They were headed to the same area of the world that Jonah had refused to go; he actually ran the other way from God's leading. But this couple were going full steam ahead with joy in their hearts. They were going to be living just a few hundred kilometers from Jonah's final destination of Ninevah.

I could tell that my grandma's heart was winning the battle over my missions-pastor's heart. The country where they were headed was embattled in war. There was a cruel dictator. There was fighting all around where they would be living.

Although they were not being sent out from our church, we did have a part in their support. The U.S. town where they lived was about an hour and a half car ride from where we lived. There was something about the seven of them that had won my heart; I admired them so much.

On the day of their departure, I asked Lynn if we could drive to the airport to see them off, and he readily agreed. When we got to the airport, they weren't there. We had just missed them, but we could see them walking through security. We caught their eye and at least got to wave them off. I laughingly told Lynn that God probably wanted to make sure I didn't take a last shot at talking them out of going.

***

The following year, we were traveling to that part of the world for our focus area and decided that we wanted to check in on how they were doing. (My grandma heart was still a little concerned for them all.)

It was not a particularly easy place to pop in to. The planes in and out of that part of the world always came and went at the weirdest times. We left very early for the airport. We landed at our destination at 4:00 AM, thus disturbing the sleep of our next host because he had to leave his house by 3:00 AM.

Getting in and out of their airport was quite a process. There were armed guards all around, and our photos were taken as we entered the waiting room hall and then taken again at passport control. Having traveled through most of the night, I am sure that our photos were not very flattering, but I am guessing that didn't matter.

Each suitcase was opened and gone through meticulously, and then we had to repack to get every item squeezed back in. I learned after 9/11, even for domestic travel, to pack in 2-gallon zip-lock bags. It helped with repacking. We were glad we had just two suitcases: one with our clothes for our four-day visit and the other with goodies for the family.

I did not have a moment of self-pity because I was thinking what that procedure had been for them, with five sleepy children in the middle of the night. My admiration for the family continued to rise.

We had such a wonderful visit with them, and our minds were put at ease as we saw how wonderfully each one had adjusted. Mom homeschooled four of the children. They were learning to play instruments, and they sang as a family. They memorized scripture and quoted it before meals as part of their daily life. We felt better about their situation as each day passed.

Their house was very large in the middle of a populated, but dusty street. Frequent dust storms swept through the area. There were many windows throughout the house, and the window frames were set into the cement walls, but with significant gaps between the walls and the window frames. Copious amounts of dust/sand came through the windows each time there was a dust storm. The dad set about fixing that!

The main pipes that brought water into the house had little to no pressure, so Dad went out to see if he could find the problem. The neighbors, who had the same problem, were curious, so the family began to meet them and make friends. Fixing water pipes or plugging holes in the gaps of the windows wasn't the translation work that he thought he was coming to do, but it was opening doors to meeting his neighbors.

The couple's hospitality was amazing. They gave us their bedroom and welcomed us in to simply do life with their family. We were able to go to an evening of worship with coworkers in their city. I remember our being introduced as their first visitors. When we visited them again, six years later, he introduced us as their second visitors. It wasn't exactly a place on a tour guide's radar.

The people there had been through a horrendous time. The previous dictator hated the nationality of these people and did his best to eradicate them. We visited a museum with the whole family on our second visit. What a somber time to walk through the building; on the ceilings and all around there were about 100,000 tiny white lights. In this place of remembrance, there is a light for each of the people who had been gassed or murdered in some way by that dictator. Each of the villages that had been decimated was represented as the name of every single person killed was read. The war that we had heard about became much more real as we heard each name and learned of the destruction that took place. The atrocities, as in several other war-torn countries, are too difficult to recount.

As we came out of the building, the tanks, anti-aircraft weapons, and armor-plated vehicles were all out in the playground. Kids in the USA have swings and seesaws to play on, but here the kids played on weapons of war.

***

One of our favorite memories of our first visit was the night we asked the children how they were liking their new house. The house, back in its time, was quite a structure, with a large marble winding staircase. The children slept upstairs on mattresses. Because of the political tension all around them, they were sometimes afraid. While we were there, campaigning for elections was going on, and there were parades, car horns honking, and loud people marching in the streets. It was a little disconcerting to the children, especially at night. Often the power went off. One of the younger children said, "When the lights go off and we can't see, and the parades and noise and guns are going off, I get scared. Mom and Dad are way downstairs, and it is so dark. Sometimes I am afraid I can't find them in the dark."

My dear husband Lynn, a missionary kid himself, to this day always has a little flashlight in his pocket. When he was growing up, the noises were of some bird or animal outside in the African bush. If he heard or saw an animal in the night, he would shine the light and check the color of the eyes to know what kind of species he was facing. There were no street lights in that part of Africa. His favorite gift to give and to get is a flashlight. We asked the kids, but, no, they didn't have flashlights.

We went to bed after talking with the kids and decided we would ask the parents if we could take the kids for ice cream the next day. Lynn's goal was to find five flashlights in the city.

The next day we went for a walk with the kids and had success! In a tiny store, we found ice cream but more importantly, Lynn found five flashlights, all different colors. They were the kind you could plug in to recharge and not have to buy batteries. These small gifts definitely felt like a God hug to us. A different color for each child! We serve the God of details.

When we had our last quiet time together, the last night we were there, Lynn talked about how important it was for them to be lights for Jesus. Their sweet nine-year-old shared that he had given his life to Jesus the previous Sunday, which was Valentine's Day. His little face beamed as he told us. Then he shared these very profound, nine-year-old thoughts about our little gift of a flashlight. "It is really important, if you want the battery charged, that you have clean connections so that you can connect to the power source. I want to have a clean heart and be connected to Jesus."

Then G, who was eight, piped in, "I think that Satan tries to corrode our batteries so that we don't get a good connection to the power source, but when we believe in Jesus, He is our power source."

Were they really only eight and nine years old? I felt like I was in a theology class in college. We went to sleep that night with a total assurance that these parents, living in a war-torn country, with challenges all around, whether the challenges were dust, water problems, or rowdy parades with horns blaring and guns going off, were doing just great. This Grandma heart of mine was perfectly at peace, remembering that the safest and best place in all the world is at the center of God's will.

This is what I remember as I pray for the next generation of the Lord's people serving one another both locally and globally.

Made in the USA
Columbia, SC
05 April 2022